/

◌

Carol Paulger
Southerly,
Morchard Bishop,
Devon.   Jan.
                2002

The Changing Year

The Changing Year

Edited by
KAREN ALEXANDER

THE FIELD

HARMSWORTH ACTIVE

Published by Harmsworth Active
10 Sheet Street, Windsor SL4 1BG, England

First published 1993

Alexander, Karen
The Changing Year.
1. Great Britain. Countryside
I. Title

British Library Cataloguing-in-Publication Data.
A catalogue record for this book is available from the British Library.

ISBN 1 873057 17 2

Printed and bound in Great Britain by
BPCC Wheatons Limited, Exeter

PREFACE

The Field has changed in many ways since 1853: it was a weekly country newspaper, and aside from the regular sporting matters of the day, it reported on weighty issues from all over the world: wars, their respective atrocities, and crime in the cities were all covered – often in gory detail. As a bit of light relief amongst the serious business, small items, diverting articles and poetry would appear. These poems were not perfectly scanned and structured, but they were written, as was everything in the magazine, out of a true love of the countryside. It is perhaps surprising how sentimental some of these pieces are, for they were written by true countrymen, who are really meant to avoid sentimentality – in public, at least.

The Field has always provided a forum for lively exchanges between warring factions over some question or other, and many of the correspondents were regulars. The magazine did not always resolve readers' questions, however (see the matter of the bullfinch), nor did it always answer them quite correctly (*vide* the letter on the grey squirrel's method of attacking the red).

It was an onerous task to choose two hundred pages of extracts from one hundred and forty years of *The Field* and produce a book that reflects the catholic tastes of its readers today. Not everyone is interested in lengthy discussions on fly-tying; numerous variations on shooting stance and how many eyes to keep open; or detailed accounts on how to breed the perfect foxhound.

It is from the light hearted pieces that I have chosen: they are both timeless and "of their time." I think many of the writers had tongue firmly in cheek, so be warned. It doesn't matter where the book is opened first, or in what order the articles are read; I hope there is something of interest, whatever one's favourite sport or pastime. Be educated, be amused, or be moved – and for true lovers of the country, make sure the latter is behind closed doors.

K.A.

Contents

CONTENTS

CONTENTS

January

A HORSE FOR KEEPING WARM
(1969)

Sir, Lucy Glitters, a seven-year-old mare, recently saved the life of 77-year-old groom, Bill Salisbury, when she lay down beside him after he had collapsed in the stables at Oak Tree Farm, Little Budworth, Cheshire. She kept him warm until found by his employer, Miss Bet Schwabe, nine hours later.

Later Mr Roger Ellams, 25, a groom at Mr Gordon Woodward's stables eight miles away at Higher Whitley, said that he trained the horse to do it whenever he went out for an evening and had too many drinks.

He said: "I used to get locked out if I was not in by midnight so I would curl up in the stable straw and encourage the mare to lie down beside me and keep me warm. I would not feel too safe among most horses but this one was very sweet natured and gentle. I am thrilled that she is carrying on the good work."

His employer, Mr Woodward, who owns hunters, show-jumpers and race horses, bought the mare in the Republic of Ireland in 1965 and named her Hard To Forget. He sold her to Miss Schwabe after three successful seasons show-jumping. Mr Ellams says that he is now trying to train Phebus Star, a six-year-old hunter, for such an emergency.

KEN OULTRAM

9

THE SPIRIT OF HOGMANAY
(1969)

The origin of Hogmanay, the ancient and peculiarly Scottish rite whose name defies derivation, lies somewhere behind the misty curtain dividing history from mythology. It is Scotland's exultation of Yule, the Roman Saturnalia, the Daft Days, the Twelve Days of Christmas, and the protracted pagan hallelujah of the winter solstice on to which the Nativity was grafted by a Christianity inspired with the thought that the birth of the solar year, long celebrated in the heathen world, was a good time to choose for the annual festival of the birth of Christ.

While the Scots are not exactly heathen it is nevertheless beyond question that to them the peak of the twelve days is Hogmanay. In the pre-Reformation era Christmas was solemnly observed in every kirk throughout the land. However, John Knox, who seems to have started where Calvin left off, believed that the celebration of Christmas, as of Easter, carried the taint of what he vilified as Roman idolatry and it was outlawed with all the rigour which that astonishing man could command.

For nearly four centuries Christmas in Scotland was just another working day, but Scots who returned from the last war brought an awareness of Christmas as being anything but just another day. Some shops and factories actually decided to close for the day, some ministers opened their kirks for Christmas services. Now, nearly all shops and factories close for the day but attendance in the kirks is still small. Not to put too fine a point upon it, Scotland's outlook on the festival remains secular.

The superstitions remain, particularly in respect of the hair colouring of first-footers. Fair-haired folk are as welcome as any, but only if they are preceded over the threshold by a dark man or woman. Some say that their superstition is derived from the rites of the Druids who blackened their heads with ashes of ceremonial bonfires as a protection against evil. Its origin could lie perhaps in the old fear and hatred of blond Norse invaders?

What is sadly dying out of Hogmanay is the ancient
guising, an inheritance from the old Celtic Hogmanay which
was at Hallowe'en. Every Scottish region had its own
tradition of guising at Hogmanay performed by young men
sometimes dressed as girls. In the North-East the Thiggar's
Chant was typical: "We wish ye a' a gude New Year,
Besouthern Besouthern, wi' worth o' health an' dainty cheer
an' awa by southron toun." After a few verses of this on the
threshold the gude wife would open the door and holding a
broom over the head of the leading guiser in a gesture of self-
defence would say "Come in, come ben, ye're welcome here
ye'll get a share o' New Year cheer, an' awa' by southron
toun." The drift of young men to the town persists and town
ways are not conducive to such cheering fancies.

Het Pint, old ale mulled and spiced, is no longer carried
through the city streets on the chime of midnight, attended
by boys ladling from the giant copper cauldrons. In the
country, brose of oatmeal, honey and whisky is not as
common as it was to our forefathers.

> 'A cogie o' yill an' a pickle oatmeal
> An' a dainty wee drappie o' whisky
> Was oor forefathers' dose for to swill down the brose
> An' keep them aye cheery an' frisky.'

H. H.-B.

THE THINKING DOG
(1942)

The embers have nearly gone out: I put on a dry piece of
birch, and soon a bright flame is flaring up. The room is cosy
and warm, smelling of pipe smoke and wet boots. My chair is
comfortable, I am pleasantly tired, and the bookshelf is within
reach of my right hand. Biggan lies close to the fire on an old
coat, warming her belly, half asleep, with her nose tucked into
her side. There may, of course, be the scent of wet dog in my

room, but this is a smell that has never worried me, and I hardly notice it nowadays, at least not as a nuisance.

Biggan is tired; we went after badger three times this week, and this evening we stayed in the duck bog until quite late. I had fastened her in the usual way during the walk-up, with the loop of her lead through my belt. Her mother would keep to heel perfectly, even on exciting occasions, but in those days I had more opportunity for concentrating on details of training. Now I don't go out so often, the belt method has succeeded the free staying to heel.

I saw no mallard – there are practically none this year – but I shot a couple of teal. One fell on the far side of the ditch. I had to go a long way to get across, but thought I had marked the bird perfectly – two trees on the edge of the wood, a particularly high post in the ditch fence, and the tall brown grassy clump where it came down.

I let Biggan off the lead and told her to seek. She cast willingly backwards and forwards, with little sniffs up and down in the clump, but after thirty seconds she seemed tired of keeping to the high grass, and set off in large bounds with her head up, further out to the side, quite a long way from the clump. I was absolutely certain of my marking – the duck was either in the clump or, if a runner, a line must be found where he had gone across the shorter grass nearby. If there is anything I hate in an experienced dog, it is carelessness, impatience, and over-keenness – all relapses to youthful faults.

My voice was sharper than usual when I rebuked her; I ordered her harshly back to the clump, and when she reached it, I kept her there with an annoyed tone in my voice, literally gluing her firmly to the eight or ten square yards of brown bog grass, breast-high. She worked, though more slowly, poking her nose into all the thick tufts and going over the whole clump time after time as methodically as ever, but I saw that she was not really trying, she was not interested, she had no use for the clump. Finally, she pulled up and looked hard at me with her small dark eyes, so full of fire and expression: for several seconds she put all the intensity of which she was capable into her stare, just standing still and boring into my eyes with her pupils. Clearly it was an attempt to talk, and it was quite superfluous when she added one or two long-drawn grunts which she uses sometimes to communicate with me. I understood at once, felt chided, and immediately let her leave the clump to go where she wanted.

She found the teal almost at once – it lay in another similar clump over a gunshot away; I had counted the posts wrongly, but soon recognised the place when I saw it.

My behaviour *was* explicable and pardonable – in a clump of very thick, coarse, and almost breast-high bog grass a duck, killed in the air, may hurtle down like a bullet and fall through many layers of half rotten dead grass, even down to the firm layer of roots in the bottom of a tuft. Its scent may, if the day is calm, remain like a narrow wisp of chimney smoke in the top of the grass four feet above the ground; it may stay like this for a long time, immobile as a pillar, without any of it being wafted down into the range of a dog who does not happen to come right up to the place; the thick grass prevents any leakage of scent to the side.

The golden rule: "If your dog's a good one, rely on him," is one that I find very difficult to put into practice; and I have heard the same thing from my shooting friends, many of whom are much better and more experienced dog people than myself.

But after Biggan's first thorough search, my excuse was hardly feasible. I had seen her work across the clump yard by yard, and burrow her nose into all the thickest tufts as well. If the dead duck had been lying there, she would have found it, if it had come down wounded and then run, she must have found the line and gone away on it with her nose to the ground, not jumping about in the way she did. On the other hand I was certain – humanly, intelligently, and superciliously dead sure, of the correctness of my exact reckoning of the line between the trees, the posts, and the clump; in such circumstances one naturally prefers to believe that "even the best dog may be out of form" than imagine the possibilities of oneself being at fault. A real dog-handler should never be guilty of this, but I often make a mess of such a situation.

Biggan had been asked many times before to hunt without success over beats where I had reason to believe game should be found, but which proved to be empty; and at the moment when she completed her second hunt (which for her had obviously been pointless all the time) and appealed to me: "Steady, old chap, listen to me a minute, don't be so unreasonable" – when she grasped that I imagined the duck was there, she understood my mistake ("Of course it's tragic he has such a bad nose!") – and forgave my stupid behaviour and mistakenly sharp tone. In other words – at that moment she knew very much better what was taking place in my mind than I knew what was going on in hers.

COUNT BJORN VON ROSEN
(Translated from the Swedish by Huldine V. Beamish)

NO MORE THE GENTLEMAN'S TIP
(1969)

Gentlemen tip half-crowns, cads only florins. Nothing separates them more certainly in the eyes of hotel doormen. This crucial test will soon be gone. The last half-crown has been minted. No more will be made because of decimalisation within two years, and there is no precise equivalent in the new coinage.

I shall be sad to see it go. The half-crown has a place in the scheme of things that no other coin can take. Since gold coinage dropped out of everyday usage, it has lorded over our small change. It is still fat enough to fill a schoolboy's palm.

Keep a weather eye open for any dated 1952. Owing to King George VI's death only a few were struck. They were withdrawn, but one is known to have escaped the melting pot.

In the West End it is still possible to buy many things for 2s 6d. Fortnum's sell all sorts. The include a portion of fruit cake, a wooden spoon, a wholemeal cob, large box of crisps, and Italian hard cheese crushed with millet seeds. At Harrods 2s 6d will buy a pet mouse, a rubber bone, a toy for your budgerigar, a box of pins, a bridge pencil set or a plastic plant.

LEADING ARTICLE

GAME FOR SHOOTERS
(1969)

Like most families, we acquire family games and they form a focal point when the horses are in, the snow is falling hard and the dog is in front of the fire. One from Australia simulated life as the owner of a sheep-station and introduced us to some entrancing diseases. It is not difficult to imagine the general idea. On the debit side, losses may occur from rabbits, droughts, bush-fires, liver-fluke and the like, but equally one may make a fortune by big clips, high wool prices, enlarged pasturage and so on.

We had staying with us a man who has several thousand merinos somewhere north of Melbourne and we made him play it. He blenched when he heard the conditions. "This is horribly lifelike," he said, but he buckled down to it and ran out an easy winner; if the game responds so readily to expert knowledge it must be a good one.

A similar type has come this year concerning the joys of keeping horses in training. I have not tried it yet, but I picked up a hazard card and found it read: "Horse pulls up sound after gallop; pay trainer £50." I have never had a horse in a racing stable, so I do not know the precise obligations of ownership, but if that is one of them why are we not all trainers?

However, few of us have sheep-stations or racehorses and the time has surely come to produce a game about a sport of which more of us have a working knowledge. I would enjoy designing one around shooting. It should not encourage competition between guns, but perhaps the owner has contracted to supply a dealer with a hundred birds and so looks to guests to shoot their quota.

One would buy cartridges initially and two barrels at a bird would be allowed twice the chance of a single shot. One might draw for dogs which could range from the proficient ("retrieves all runners") via the opportunist ("at each stand brings in one bird shot by a neighbouring gun") to the shameful ("chases hare into covert and flushes birds; pay other guns").

There would be hazard cards – "forgotten to buy a Game Licence," "pepper passing police car" or "left sandwiches at home and shoot badly" – all invoking calculated penalties, but there would also be compensating advantage cards – "draw best place at best stand," "at top of one's form" or "port after luncheon makes one shoot like Annie Oakley for one drive."

I cannot quite see how it would all work out, but if anybody else can I shall be delighted to test it out on the family and forward their blunt comments. It is time we consumed our national smoke and ceased to borrow from the ends of the earth in order to find entertainment in the contemplation of the dangers of pulpy kidney in our flocks.

C. C. L. BROWNE

LICENCES FOR MOTOR CAR DRIVERS
(1902)

One of the most useless and unnecessary restrictions with which it has been sought to hamper and harass automobilists is that which has reference to the licensing of the drivers of motor-cars after applying some test of competency. That it has been devised mainly with a hostile intent and not in deference to the safety of the public is obvious to any observer of the skill with which motor-cars are customarily managed and guided on the public roads.

The cleverest coachman who ever handled a whip, with the best trained horses, could not guide and control the movements of the vehicle he drives with anything like the accuracy that is exhibited by the comparative novices in automobilism. We all know that the skill often shown by the drivers of horses is such as to excite admiration, but whatever his skill, the driver is always, to some extent, at the mercy of his horse, the vagaries of which are liable to upset the best calculations. When the lever or steering wheel is substituted for the reins in the guidance of a vehicle a positive result is obtained. There is no doubt or hesitancy as to the effect that will be produced, for there is no intermediary to be reckoned with, and the driver is able to give his undivided attention to what is going on around him. Unlimited brake power is at his instant service by the pressure of his foot upon a lever, so that his control of the vehicle is full and complete.

It is difficult to reconcile this demand for exacting from the automobilist a test of competency with the indifference that is exhibited to the absence of skill or knowledge that is so marked a characteristic of the drivers of horses in certain classes of traffic. The tradesman's cart, for instance, is entrusted to any youth who applies for the situation, quite irrespective of his qualifications for the office, and possibly the first time he takes a pair of reins in his hands he is sent out into the crowded streets of a town in charge of a horse, of whose peculiarities he is quite ignorant. He is assumed to know the rule of the road; if not, he acquires the knowledge at his own expense or, more often, at the expense of someone else. His experience is developed on the lines of expediency, as witness the way in which he systematically cuts corners whether he be turning to the left or the right. This class of driver, whose methods are adopted by many others who also have had no tuition, is a menace to the safety of town and suburban streets, and many accidents for which he provides the essentials are only averted by the extra care and skill exercised by others. It would be a *reductio ad absurdum* to leave such drivers as these to a free and unfettered misuse of the roads while exacting from others, whose competence is obvious to all, an official demonstration of efficiency in the control of the vehicles. When proposals such as this and the reduction of speed to ten miles an hour come to be examined on their merits their inconsistency is apparent, and their only effect is to shake the confidence of the public in the sincerity of other and less unreasonable demands for the regulation of motor-car traffic which emanate from the same quarter.

Upon the question of speed we may be considered to be within measureable distance of unanimity, for the clerk to the Gloucestershire County Council, in his communication to the Local Government Board states, in explanation of the suggestion for the removal of the speed limit, that the primary object of the proposed alterations is to place the responsibility for the speed on the drivers of motor-cars themselves. In the opinion of his council the present limit of speed is generally disregarded by motor-car drivers, and can only be enforced with very great difficulty, while the safety of the speed at which motor-cars are driven is so entirely dependent upon the various circumstances and localities that no fixed scale of speed can be made which would be suitable to all circumstances and places. These eminently sensible remarks may be taken as fairly representing the views we have frequently expressed, as well as those held by people who have calmly examined the question in all its bearings.

H. GRAVES

THE CANON'S WILD GOOSE CHASE
(1960)

My wildfowling companion switched the light on over my bed and informed me that it was a wild morning, that there would be a cup of tea ready downstairs in five minutes and that he had been outside already and heard the geese in the distance.

Once or twice a year he is able to snatch a few days from his clerical duties – he is a Canon of the Church of England– to go wildfowling; and Captain Ahab's fanatical pursuit of the white whale, Moby Dick, was child's play compared to my friend's wild-goose chases. My enthusiasm has dwindled with increasing years and as I heard the wind and struggled into my storm-resisting clothes, I remembered the remark of an old Scottish gamekeeper, toiling over the heather on a dirty day: "Call this work and wha would do it?"

As the hot tea is gulped down we cram our pockets with cartridges, the big stuff for the geese in one and the smaller for the duck in another. The kitchen fire never goes out here and the place is like an oven, but when the door is opened we are met by a blast of wind right off the North Sea and gasp for breath. Then we are on the move, full of that hopeful anticipation which to my mind is the best part of wildfowling.

It is still dark and we have to feel our way out of the backyard of the inn through inches of black, slippery mud and a litter of pig troughs, chicken-coops and dog-kennels. There is a noise like castanets coming from the shed; the corrugated-iron sheets are flapping in the gale and a bantam cock challenges us from an elder-bush growing through a hole in the roof. The pigs, too, want to know who is about and complain that they are hungry.

There is a choice of ways out: one can either negotiate an entanglement of barbed wire or take the longer way through a gate that tests the length of one's waders with smelly mud: I shouldn't want to fall down here. Having reached the footpath in safety, the Canon goes off at a half walk, half trot; I and my arthritic leg follow at my own pace.

To reach my favourite spot in the dyke behind the present sea wall, there are two earlier walls to cross and it is interesting to see the amount of land that has been reclaimed and how far the salt water has been pushed back; one large building, still known as Island Farm, now stands well inland, though below sea-level. Geese graze in peace on these flats for they can see all round and are unapproachable; they have not far to fly for a drink and some sharp sand for their gizzards.

By the time I am settled among the reeds there is a glimmer of light in the east; gulls fly silently in formation like geese; curlew slip by, invariably when I am looking the other way, and what a variety of calls they have, all full of music, but some derisive. A barn owl beats up and down the dykes, right to where I am waiting; while one of its relatives, a short-eared owl, fans some rushy grass with its long wings in the hope of exposing a mouse or some small bird.

All sorts of things pass through my mind as I wait. Where has that parson got to? I have not heard him shoot. What are they doing at home? – as if I cared! Is my gun safe? Where shall I face? There is two-way traffic here, the geese going in one direction, the ducks in another, diametrically opposite.

Of course, the wind has dropped by now – it always does – and everything will be up in the stratosphere. What has happened to the geese? If they are still the other side of the sea-wall they must all have their heads tucked under their wings and be fast asleep. But no, not all, because I hear a "Quink, quink" from a pink-footed goose. Then all is quite again until an old gander suddenly give the order "Wakey! Wakey!" The loud, commanding "Ag-ank!" is followed by that stirring and wonderful chorus that never fails to thrill me as several thousand geese lift and take off, skein after skein, for the Wolds in the opposite county.

But my waiting time has not been wasted, though I have not fired a shot. I have heard and seen the geese; I have seen the dawn, the sky changing from apple-green through all the shades of mauve, orange and red; and I have seen a bird that is new to me, a rough-legged buzzard, which was being mobbed by starlings, fieldfares and blackbirds. Besides all that, a little merlin flew quite close and it was amusing to see its amazing acceleration when it caught sight of me.

I am wondering what there is for breakfast, a thing I never do at home! The sun is not yet high enough for me to see it over the skyline of the opposite Wolds, but the incoming duck, high in the air, can see it and their breasts are rose-tinted from its reflection. Presently a dot in the distance turns out to be the Canon, swinging a mallard in one hand, an unlucky bird that for some unaccountable reason has been low enough for him to shoot.

The local lock-keeper was a noted wildfowler and our very good friend, and if he heard us shoot and saw us looking for a bird, he would send Old Ben over to assist us. Ben was an outsized Labrador, with feet as wide as my hand and semi-webbed; he had retrieved hundreds of geese in his time and never failed us, but he had a penchant for taking everything to his master. To see Ben gallop back home with six or seven pounds of goose was a sight to remember. Sometimes, whether we liked it or not, the little black bitch Sooty from the inn would accompany us, but she was more interested in the ground game than the wildfowl.

We potter about all day and his Reverence shoots a pheasant or two for our host, on whose farm we have been (and who does not carry a gun often, but when he does he shuts both eyes when he pulls). We have no better luck than in the morning, but just as I am preparing for bed, the indefatigable one looks out of the window, catches a glimpse of the moon between the clouds and begins to put on his wildfowling kit and reach for his gun. He returns at 2.15 with a young pink-footed goose. He is satisfied with just one or two, but does not like to return home empty-handed.

S. AUBREY SEYMOUR

THE WILD GEESE
(1923)

Had I not seen, against the glowing light
Of dusk, a wedge of wild geese in their flight,
And heard their clamour – Ah, that magic cry –
Clear in the frosty stillness, haply I
Had settled in the fireside chair, intent
On musty tomes of legal precedent.

But now there comes and comes and comes to me
The crooning and the murmur of the sea,
An hour before the dawn, at flighting time,
A Winter dawn; my greatcoat white with rime,
When, crouching low behind the grey sea-wall
I waited for the geese, and heard their call.

W. G. M. DOBIE

February

CARE FOR A COCKATOO?
(1969)

Sir, When a friend was going to Africa, she asked my aunt if she would care for her cockatoo while she was gone. It would be a companion for my aunt's parrot. After a while the parrot died, and the cockatoo, Kikee, became sad and lonely.

One morning a rat was seen under the table of Kikee's cage. Rats were not allowed into the house and it was hoped that either the cats or the stable lad would kill it. I had other ideas as, when going late to bed, I would hear faint murmurings from Kikee and guessed she was calling the rat. A week or so later I heard rather a lot of murmuring and scuffling, so I very quietly lifted the cover to peer in. The rat and Kikee were sitting close together on the perch, undisturbed by my curiosity. The murmurings became like a cat purring and the rat never failed to turn up three or four nights a week.

Friends used to come from far and wide to witness this strange friendship. Kikee became so happy that she laid an egg (when she was about 21). She didn't quite know what to do with it and pushed it round the floor of the cage.

Joan C. Stevens

THE BULLFINCH
(1860)

A handsome, well-known bird is the bullfinch. His plumage, of almost tropical colouring, renders him a beautiful and conspicuous object in wood, field, orchard, garden and plantation. Although far from uncommon, more than two are rarely seen together; but it more frequently occurs that only a solitary bird is observed (usually in some field or rural lane), flitting along in short low flights from bush to bush.

During the breeding season, the bullfinch is truly arboreal in his habits, hiding himself in the depths of thickly-foliaged woods, and being rarely seen. As winter approaches, however, he leaves these retreats, and is a constant visitor to gardens and orchards. This occurs most frequently about February. They inflict considerable injury upon the budding trees. They prefer the buds of the cherry, plum, damson and gooseberry, rather avoiding those of the currant, apple and pear. Stone-fruit tree-buds are their choice favourites. I have seen a single bird strip more than a dozen twigs in a very short space of time: he commenced at the bottom of each twig, twisting off every bud until he arrived at the top, when he moved to another. They certainly prefer the blossom buds. To young plantations they are very destructive, and it is found necessary in such cases to thin them down year by year. The bullfinch also eats various kinds of berries and wild fruits, and the leaves of the groundsel and other plants.

The nest, usually built in a wood or plantation, is placed four or five feet from the ground, in some bush or tree, and is composed externally of twigs and lined with roots and moss. Incubation lasts about a fortnight, the young leaving the nest towards the middle of June. The male and female birds relieve each other whilst sitting upon the eggs, the male bird occasionally solacing his better half with a song when it becomes her turn to occupy the nest. Both birds when sitting upon eggs have been found so tame as to allow themselves to be stroked down the back by the hand, without manifesting the slightest fear. The bullfinch has occasionally, if not always, two broods in a season.

It will breed in confinement, as illustrated by the following note from a writer in the *Zoologist*: "In the spring of 1837, a pair of these birds, which had been caged some months, were observed eagerly picking up moss and hair in the room in which they were accustomed to fly loose, and on their being furnished with materials speedily constructed a nest, chiefly of fibrous roots, similar to that of the bullfinch in a state of nature. The female laid five eggs, from which three young birds were hatched; they appeared to thrive well for ten days, the old birds feeding them regularly on egg boiled hard, but at the end of that time they suddenly forsook them, perhaps from the want of insect food. In consequence of this desertion two of the young birds died, but the third was saved, being brought up in a nest of young canaries."

The bullfinch is a very fair songster, and in confinement may be educated to sing popular airs. There are few persons who, some time or other, have not fallen in with a piping bullfinch – the pet of a household. These birds, however, are sometimes capricious, and refuse to sing at the very time when their notes are most desired to be heard.

A poor woman of my acquaintance had once a piping bullfinch, who, on account of his cleverness, was a somewhat remarkable character. His manners and habits had been her amusement and solace for many a long hour, and he was high in favour with his mistress. The lady of a neighbouring mansion called one day at the woman's cottage and heard him perform a solo. Being struck with his performance, and being particularly fond of birds, she set her heart upon possessing the pet. A guinea was offered and at first refused; but the woman was poor – money was tempting. A winter-store of coals or a piping bullfinch, which would she possess? Poverty pulled hard at her apron-string and whispered in her ear: "a guinea is a guinea – you can get another bird next year." Tommy was sold, and Tommy was duly delivered at his new abode. His old wooden cage was exchanged for one of brass wire, which seemed to astonish him by its glittering splendour. If he had been heir to a dukedom his daily wants could not have been better supplied. To him was given the purest water and the choicest seed, and when in return for all her attention his kind-hearted mistress expected a song, no song came forth. He who had been the delight of his cage of a cottage would not sing in his gaudy palace. Tommy was as mute as a snowflake. What was to be done? His piping had induced his mistress to buy him, but since he would not pipe he had no value in her eye. So she returned Master Tommy to his original owner, but did not receive the guinea in return. Located once more in his old cage and in his old quarters, the gentleman regained his spirits and resumed his song, and long continued to gladden the home which the lady's liberality had made more bright.

JOHN JOSEPH BRIGGS, F.R.S.L.

Sir, In last Saturday's Field *a correspondent calls the bullfinch a pest of the garden. Might I beg of that gentleman and any others that have the opportunity, to take notice of those trees and bushes that are attacked by the bullfinches, and compare the quantity of fruit borne on them and on others, when not operated on by the despised bullfinches. My experience, drawn from several years' observation, has convinced me that the bullfinches' visits are more beneficial than injurious; I allude to their bud-picking propensity. I have seen gooseberry bushes and plum and cherry trees completely stripped of their buds, and yet on those trees a much larger crop of fruit than in years when they were not visited by the persecuted birds. I can only suggest that the buds being eaten off causes the tree to bloom later, having to form fresh buds, and so the fruit escapes the late frosts.*

B. P. BRENT

Sir, A writer in the Field *has, I think, fallen into the common error of confounding the post hoc with the ergo propter hoc. Bullfinches are notorious for attacking the buds which contain blossoms, not those which contain leaves only; but as the former are invariably found during the previous summer, it is utterly impossible for a tree that has been despoiled of all of them to bear any fruit: the tree has not the power of forming a second set.*

C. A. J.

Sir, C. A. J. says that I have fallen into an error respecting the destruction caused by bullfinches to fruit trees. All I ask is that he and other denouncers of this persecuted bird suspend judgment till they can prove their theories by careful observation.

As to C. A. J.'s assertion that it is utterly impossible for a tree that has been despoiled of all buds to bear fruit is disproved by the facts: as the greengage tree, to which I have particularly alluded, and which I minutely examined, had not any buds remaining, neither blossom nor leaf buds, yet that tree bloomed freely and bore an excellent crop of fruit that same season.

Nor is C. A. J.'s theory that the tree has not the power of forming a second set of buds borne out in practice. Gardeners, when they desire to throw extra strength into any particular bud, will rub off those around, but this will not prevent the sockets whence those buds have been removed from putting forth fresh buds; those sockets contain the germ of several buds which, when the principal are destroyed, others are developed. The idea that the trees may bloom more profusely next year on account of having been stripped of their buds is, I think, not improbable; for the retarding of the trees by the stripping them of buds would be likely to induce that stunted or short-jointed growth which, in many kinds, produces the most fruit. Thus, it may be that the bullfinches not only do no harm, but are positively beneficial.

B. P. BRENT

THE PIGEONS OF GUILDHALL
(1860)

At a committee of Aldermen, held at Guildhall, Alderman Wilson having represented that Wm. Temple, the hall-keeper, had given directions to some of the persons in waiting upon the several committees, to destroy the pigeons which have been sheltered by the nooks and crannies of the buildings for many years, and have of late become exceedingly numerous, that officer was called before the Aldermen, to account for having issued an order so much at variance with the taste of the Corporation.

The hall-keeper said the inhabitants of King-street, Cheapside, in the immediate vicinity of the Guildhall, had often complained of the pigeons, a nuisance of which none but those who were subjected to their frequent visits could form an adequate opinion.

Alderman Wilson. – I should wish to have some instances in which the poor pigeons have given such mortal offence. – (Hear, hear.) Sir James Shaw, our old Chamberlain, with whose kindness of heart we are all acquainted, took great delight in supplying them with food, considering that it was essential to the character of the Guildhall for hospitality that such harmless tenants should receive a little of the bounty of the Corporation.

The hall-keeper said that about three or four years ago the splendid dress of a lady who sat at the Lord Mayor's dinner in the hall was completely destroyed by the unceremonious conduct of some of the pigeons above her head. – (Laughter.) Two years ago, when his own servant girl went into one of the bedrooms, she was terrified by a noise in the chimney, and immediately afterwards down tumbled a quantity of soot, and a pigeon in the midst of it. But that was not the only disagreeable consequence of the unwelcome visit, for the bird in its flight fluttered not only against the walls of the room, but against the curtains of the bed, and did a great deal of damage. The whole room was covered with soot. – (Laughter.)

Alderman Lawrence. – It seems, then, that the pigeon saved you the expense of employing a chimney-sweeper. It is quite evident, from the quantity of soot which accompanied the bird on its visit to your bedroom, that you don't lay out much money in carrying out that portion of our sanitary regulations. – (Laughter.)

The hall-keeper. – The passages to my house are constantly covered with dirt from the multitude. I am sure I would be obliged to any one who would kill them.

Alderman Cubitt said, at Venice and Constantinople pigeons were so much respected, that they were maintained at the public expense, and nobody was permitted to molest them. He could not see why the Guildhall pigeons, which had, as it were, become part and parcel of the Corporation, should be disturbed, except, indeed, to make pies of them for the use of the Corporation. (Great laughter.)

Alderman Humphrey said, he thought the hall-keeper could give the committee a very fair idea of the flavour of the birds, as he had so great an anxiety to put them to death.

The hall-keeper. – I assure you, sir, that I never tasted one of them in my life.

Alderman Wilson. – We will certainly not allow a wholesale destruction of the pigeons, which are objects of interest in the neighbourhood, and have been, all of them, born under and upon the roof of this building.

After some further conversation, in the course of which it was generously admitted that it would be very proper to dispense with the presence of the pigeons, the hall-keeper succeeded so far in substantiating his complaint as to obtain from the committee their consent to decrease the number of the offenders to about a moiety. It was agreed that the argument of the injury to the ladies' dresses, not to say a word about the beards and bald heads of the ambassadors, and the wigs of the bishops, and judges, and sergeants learned in the law, was fatal to the cause of the birds, which were said from their chattering and cooing to take delight in the mischief they dropped upon "their magnificences" below.

ANON.

THE DONE THING AT CRUFT'S
(1969)

At Cruft's, perhaps more than at any other show, handlers take the eye almost as much as the dogs do.

English setter handlers drop on one knee beside their exhibits, arms spreadeagled to extend muzzles and tails. This shows dogs as well as lady owners to advantage. It is therefore puzzling to see a Labrador accompanied by someone affecting a Statue of Liberty pose and holding liver and biscuit aloft. The aim is to maintain the dog's head in the correct position.

Golden retrievers apparently should circle the ring four times running while handlers, mostly ladies, become pinker and more confused. Paradoxically the speedy whippets are never led out at a pace smarter than their owners' corkscrew walk. A higher speed distracts the judge.

The long-haired breeds are constantly brushed. Ringlets are undesirable. Light relief is provided by a handler's dress. One may appear in black chiffon and gold sandals, like an inmate of a harem. Sometimes an exhibitor of King Charles spaniels dresses as Charles I, the saluki handler may turn up disguised as an Arab layabout or a bloodhound will be accompanied by Sherlock Holmes.

A handler's clothes can help the exhibit. For example, a brindle dog tends to fade into Olympia's dark background. Handler's remedy: wear bright scarlet to show up the animal. Or choose a gaily coloured lead. Particolours lose outline against patterns, which should be kept for solid-coloured animals.

Bad show technique can mar a perfect dog and an unremarkable animal is often helped by astute handling. Americans recognize this and use professionals. Here and on the Continent the owner-handler is much more evident. Perhaps this contributes to their fascination.

London Diary

DOGS THAT EAT FRUIT AND SING
(1969)

Sir, With regard to Mr Bernard's letter (30 January) my whippet, a dog of 20 months, who is fed on raw meat and biscuits, eats many vegetables and different kinds of fruit; he will take raspberries and blackberries off the plant; he cracks open beans and peas, eating both contents and shell; he also takes carrots, cooking apples, brussel sprouts, raw potatoes, and artichokes from the baskets in the kitchen in which they are collected.

This omnivorous diet does not detract from his ferocious catching of hares and rabbits. My mother's Jack Russell bitch is also like this to a lesser extent. She "sings" whenever the Forsyte Saga starts, or when we put on the Moonlight Sonata. She will not let me play two notes on the piano before she howls me down.

EDWARD WODEHOUSE

Sir, Regarding Mr Wodehouse's letter (27 February), my old Labrador's favourites are gooseberries which he picks carefully from the bushes. When the siren goes to alert the fire brigade, both Labradors start to sing at the top of their voices form their kennels and so does the working terrier in the house. The terrier also sings when the telephone bell goes, but barks at door bells.

F. LONGDEN SMITH

PINS FOR DINNER
(1935)

Sir, I have a kennel of cocker spaniels, and have owned the dog in question for three years. I bought him as an eleven month old pup, and even then his passion for anything small and shiny was obvious. At first he was content to catch flies and play for hours with the same one, all the time keeping it quite unharmed, but in the last two years his passion has increased alarmingly.

Needles, pins of all kinds, buttons, razor blades, studs, screws, tacks and, his favourite of all, the tin clips on the ends of shoe laces.

I find it hard to remember half of the things he has found from time to time, and, if not pounced upon at once, all are consumed without any apparent harm, and certainly with great enjoyment. Bones and biscuits mean nothing to him. Offer him the choice of a biscuit or a bead (preferably very small) and he will choose the bead every time. I honestly believe that he would sell his soul for a card of pins.

He is in the pink of condition and shot over every week, but I must confess that keeping my eye on him takes up a good part of my time.

D. MOORE SMITH

WIGS ON THE ICE
(1969)

The wintry spell in London produced its compensations. I am told (and I prefer to believe it) that behind the crypt in Lincoln's Inn, for instance, respected members of the Bar recaptured their youth on a lethal-looking slide.

Judges, benchers and barristers, whose public mien is irreproachably solemn, abandoned decorum. Wigs were seen to fly and the cloister calm echoed to boyish shouts of "It's my turn" from stuff gownsmen (who normally waive precedence to silks) or "You rotter, Judge, you're wearing hob-nailed boots."

The slide was most popular at mid-morning and was said to measure more than 30 ft. It was made by porters using pails of water which froze quickly. Some counsel claim it was the best slide in London. The same spot in summer is reserved (they say) for stump cricket played by silks.

A LONDON DIARY

THE PERFECT MARRIAGE
(1969)

I had carved the chickens, circulated with the rum-ration, grabbed a drumstick and associated vegetables for myself and was trying to catch up with the rest of the luncheon party when my neighbour started off: "Did you grow those snowdrops?" she asked, indicating the bowl on the table. I nodded briefly, having an over-full mouth.

"Quite charming!" she said, "Those dots of white in a sea of dark green are like an ermine cape in reverse. Dark spots on a white background," she explained, in case I thought that a stoat in winter plumage had green patches on it. "Don't tell me that you arranged them too! I have a feeling that the credit is your wife's." I agreed that she had plonked them into water. "I thought so," she said. "Intuition is seldom wrong," and she had a biff at a potato.

At the other end of the table, my wife was being asked if the market was good this year for snowdrops. "Quite reasonable, I think," she answered. "But how did you know we sent them to market?" Her questioner gave a loud, male laugh.

"By a logical inference. Nobody would assemble 40 or 50 bunches, each of two dozen snowdrops and three ivy leaves if they weren't for sale. Those will all go away tomorrow. I've done it myself so I can recognize your husband's handiwork," and he chivvied a pea round his plate.

So there you have the old battle logic versus intuition, with both liable to be off-target if not blended. The simple truth was that I had cosseted them while growing, both of us had picked them and both had bunched the slippery, little things. It makes one think that if women had more logic and men more intuition we would all call our shots more correctly.

C. C. L. BROWNE

NOSE BOUND HORIZONS
(1942)

Early evening and a steady drizzle. On such a day a year ago we were again thinking of letting our cottage. It is a state of mind into which we relapse periodically. The last time we succumbed to this recurrent fever we had various applicants, and it is about one of them I wish to tell. In one sense we have been quite fortunate with such applicants; some of what are known as the best people have had the desire to spend a portion of their presumably luxurious lifetime on this sunny, rainy, hot, cold and windswept hillside of ours. When I say the best people I do not wish to imply that others are morally not just as good, or bad, for that matter; no, I merely mean the best *off* – unless, of course, Mayfair addresses are no criteria. Frankly, it rather puzzles me why Mayfair should seemingly hanker after modest little places like ours; sheer snobbishness, I suspect.

I have noticed that when, in conversation with new acquaintances, I happen to mention that we have a cottage, they at once ask where; and on hearing the word "Sussex" their demeanour becomes a shade more respectful. Since then I have on occasion tried it with "Essex," and found that was accepted as a statement of a rather regrettable geographical fact. Sussex apparently is a county where even the best people can own up to possessing a cottage; whilst in Devonshire, for example, one *must* have one's place; Scotland, it seems, is almost as entirely given up to estates as Cannes is to villas; but never mention your *villa* in an English county – that would be equivalent to social hari-kari! One may confess to owning something in Lancashire, but had better not go into details. Cornwall and the Cotswolds go down well with people who fancy the purlieus of Chelsea and Bloomsbury. I might go on mentioning localities which stamp one indelibly with a mark of social quality or mental capacity.

It is ridiculous how one judges by such geographic irrelevancies. I, too, have sinned in this respect. Years ago I met an Englishman in Brittany, a most difficult thing to avoid in those days, who, after the manner of his kind, wore cricket attire; that is to say, white flannels and a dark blue blazer, but most strikingly emblazoned, enough to make the Garter-King-at-Arms murmur his strange motto, *miserere mei Deus*, in sheer envy. I could not help inquiring which college this particular blazon signified. "LCC Shoreditch" came the prompt reply, and, snob that I am, though honest, I must confess to having experienced a sudden attack of "that sinking feeling." I have no undue respect for "the old school tie" kind of thing, so the LCC might have passed; but "Shoreditch" was too much.

Our applicant was not a denizen of Mayfair. He came from what is known as a residential suburb of London, a suburb of the more "select" kind. He had money; you could tell that by the bellyband of his cigar; but as another one, a particularly ingenuous one of that ilk, once assured me: "It's quite easy making money – you don't need any brains; it just comes of its own accord, once you've made a start."

The greyness of the afternoon and the steady downpour made our situation "on the borders of Ashdown Forest" look not quite so "beautiful" as it did in the house agent's records. Consequently, our aspirant's spirits were decidedly low. The premises, though faithfully described as a cottage, disappointed him, mainly because they lacked what he called servants' quarters. By this time I was beginning to wish he would betake himself elsewhere. So I explained, with as much dignity as I could command, that we in the country still adhered to the old feudal custom, in other words that we shared the board, sitting above the salt of course, with our retainers, a custom we found the more to our liking as we had no retainers.

I had hoped by means of my oblique oration to make him scowl and depart. Instead, he stood still and stared gloomily out of the window into the rain. Suddenly a light illumined his features – so far as that was possible. He looked intently at something in the garden. Touching my arm with one hand and pointing with the other to the lawn, "Tell me," he said, "what is the purpose of those little mounds of earth you have distributed on your lawn?" I looked at him out of the tail of my eye, thinking: "Now he is trying to get his own back; he has a sense of humour after all. I quite like him. I'll ask him to stay for tea." But there was no sign of humour, none of malice even in his guileless face. I asked, just to make sure: "Are you making fun of my lawn?" "No, why?" was the evidently surprised reply, evidently, for he gazed at me with such limpid blue-eyed innocence as only a child of four could assume or a fool of forty display.

"Oh! those mounds. I'll explain; you see I am a writer of sorts; a kind of Autolycus. I snap up and vend my little stock of unconsidered trifles. That is where *she* comes in." My visitor pricked up his ears. "You see," I continued, "she is a friend of mine, a shy creature who spends most of her time in her shelter, where she keeps herself busy, always out of my sight. She has a pink nose and small eyes and pink little hands, and with these, when I'm not looking, she shovels up the earth under the lawn and pushes it right up through the grass, thereby making visible that which otherwise would have remained unseen. *Talpa* is her name; *Talpa Europoea* to be exact, and to us in the country her little mounds are known as molehills, and they're the stuff I make my living out of – mountains I make out of molehills. Have I made myself clear?" He was not amused; he took his hat and his departure in a dudgeon of more than molehill dimensions.

That is my story – nothing much – but the moral! A man of forty or more, a man who had manifestly made money; had got on in the world; yet he did not know a molehill when he saw one. Is it we, I ask you, we who make mountains out of molehills who have done the world so much harm, or is it men like him who do not know a molehill when they see one? Or worse; is it not these others who would fain reverse our practice and make molehills out of mountains, out of volcanoes? A Mount Vesuvius, in eruption before their eyes, belching smoke and slavering lava; and they say: "Bah, 'tis nothing; a slight upheaval; it will subside."

Or, like passengers in the North Atlantic, anxious to cross "the herring pond"; they will glance at white specks on the horizon, no greater than molehills, and they will say, stout fellows, to the captain: "Surely you are not going to alter course for that? We shall lose time, Captain, and time is money, Captain!" They know not what lies hidden – even under a molehill; they cannot see beyond or below their nosebound horizons!

Forgive me, won't you? Put it down to that early evening and the steady drizzle.

Herbert Furst

PIGEONS
(1954)

'Twixt the ending of the pheasants and beginning of the trout,
There's a horrible hiatus, sent by Providence, no doubt,
To exercise the patience of a country-living chap –
But the wary, scary,
February
Pigeon fills the gap.

When the snipe and 'cock are over, and you itch to have a throw
At the salar, or the trutta, or the lively fario,
There might be a time of waiting which was troublesome to kill –
But the wary, scary,
February
Pigeon fits the bill.

When there's little in the larder, and the joint's not over big,
You could manage very nicely if you only had a pig
But you haven't, so you squander all the cartridges you've got
On the wary, scary
February
Pigeon for the pot.

L. N. JACKSON

March

NETTLES
(1942)

Sir, At the end of a long drawn out, severe winter not only does the mortality rate rapidly rise, but many ailments which do not prove fatal are prevalent and they destroy much of the Joy of Living!

And what a joy the spring-time is, if only one can wake up each morning ready to leap out of bed and hail the glory of the eastern sky ablaze with silver and gold!

Now for those who have come "under the weather" of the winter, there is no medicine to equal what our great-grandmothers called:

The spring time Saladies
To cure all winter Maladies.

Today these treasures of healing and of life-giving powers are round us peeping up in every odd corner and rubbish heap. They are the anathema of the gardener; the salvation of the anæmic - the common stinging nettle tops!

Go out gloved. Take a basket and a big pair of scissors. Cut off the tender tops, plunge into cold water and wash. Then put them dripping wet into a little saucepan. Put on the lid and shake them occasionally as they cook.

Within 20 minutes you have a delightful dish. Eat with butter or oil and perhaps the rare poached egg, and you have begun a course of hedgerow physic which will lead you towards that effervescent vitality which makes you sing in your cold bath!

JOSHUA OLDFIELD

THE YEOMAN
(1942)

The history of our English yeoman, from the Saxon Heptarchy to the Victorian Enclosures which so crippled him, is a series of variations upon a single theme which can be summed up in two Saxon monosyllables – self-help. During the Victorian period, self-help became a term of derision among the intellectuals until in our own day it has become one of those little words that, like a threepenny bit, has got lost down some grating of the pavements.

By a chance felicity, I became possessed the other day, through the kindness of a Cornish correspondent, of a most charming piece of evidence as to the yeoman's self-help in eighteenth century Cornwall. This is a duodecimo manuscript book on hand-made paper in a brown cover, stitched together, written by a yeoman in the neighbourhood of Morwenstow in 1749, "William Brimscombe his hand and his pen amen." In beautiful clear handwriting, the booklet gives a series of home-made recipes for the sickness of livestock, compounded by himself out of his own herb-garden, medicine chest and what in places reads uncommonly like a witch's cauldron. Here is one of a drench for a horse with the glanders: "Take a quart of white wine finiger and five eggs and one ounce of datapenty and five cloos of garlick put this in to a wuart cup and stop it close and put it in to a horse's dunghill that is new and hot and let it bide two hours and then give it to the horse and ride him after drenching but be sure to kepe him in that day and night."

Here is another: "If you have a horse that hath strained his shoulder let him blead in the plate vain take some oil of tepenton and oil of Spuke and anoint his shoulder well with it. If he be strained in the stifle or in the whirl bone take black sope and the joyce of Cammill and a dram of saffark and boil it in brandy or rum and anoint the place with it." And yet the moderns dare to look down on the days when brandy could be used for external applications for a horse's strain!

"Cammill" was a Somerset dialect form of camomile, and "Spuke" was Devon vernacular for lavender. "Datapenty" appears to be a composition of five ingredients, an old electuary consisting of diatessaron (which contains four ingredients, electuary of gentian, birthwort, bayberries and myrrh) with another drug added. "Saffark" is probably saffarn, a variant of saffron which, according to the OED is either *crocus metallorum vel antimonii, crocus verneris* (copper) or *crocus martis* (iron).

A descendant of this most worthy apothecary-yeoman married Richard Woodley of Hill Park, and from the marriage descended James Woodley who, in the middle of the nineteenth century, wrote a farm account book in which it appears that a bag of dredge corn cost 6/5, a bag of barley 7/-, and a bag of wheat 7/-. Among these business-like entries are three charms, most curious and enlightening. Here is one of them, written in 1845 when Hawker was Vicar of Morwenstow: "Charm for a Thorn. As Christ went over Willows Bridge he Pricked himself with a thorn he said to himself though shalt neither wrinkel nor ache so shall thy leg neither rot wrinkel nor ache so shall thy Leg Be well James Woodley in the name of the Father and of the Son and of the holy ghost."

Most of our ancient village festivals, games and observances at certain seasons of the year were, of course, a compound of pagan and Christian elements, and it is easy enough to separate the one from the other. In one the pagan background will be dominant, in another the Christian foreground, so that the expert geologist of folklore is able to view the different formations as strata regularly disposed along the rock-face of antiquity. But the interest of these unique charms (at any rate, I have never read anything like them), is that sympathetic magic and Christian faith are so completely blended that it is impossible to disentangle the one from the other.

They are, in fact, an extremely striking example of that tenacity in folk-memory which peasant and yeoman shared between them throughout long ages. Folk-memory is a communal inheritance, so that in this faded writing, the one a century and the other two centuries ago, I have before me a kind of by-ways manifestation of co-operation and self-help in harness together.

I am glad to have tracked down some of the herbal and chemical distillations of this self-helping and self-learning old yeoman, living in the backwoods of Cornwall, because, though a little of romantic bloom may be rubbed off his mysterious terminology, his stature grows rather than is dwarfed by our discovery of what he meant by it. It is clear that William Brimscombe was a man of science in the days before knowledge had become the monopoly of a few experts, to the dire consequence of their arrogance and the rest of the world's ignorance. As this "rest of the world" has lost responsibility, so together with its liberties it has lost direct experience, and I should say, without the slightest hesitation, that the average man of a couple of centuries ago, though he might have been unable to read or write, had incomparably more general knowledge of his own and his fellows' occupations than "the man in the street" of to-day has of anything outside the newspaper headline or the radio. The modern mass-mind obtaining its knowledge at second or third-hand, and having it pumped in by propaganda or popular manuals without acquiring it by experience, is probably the worst educated in the fundamentals and realities of life in the history of the world.

Another thing lost to modern life is the value of words; in variety, in texture and quality, and in meaning. A simple example will suffice – the word "sportsdrome," a word whose barbarism is based both on ignorance and lack of taste, destroyed by industrialism. In contradistinction to it, I give here some names I have recently collected for the smallest pig in the litter – doll, squab, cad, cadma, caddying, tiddling, dilling, Antony or Tony, nestle or nisgal, dawling, coacher, crank or crink, piggy-whidden, krute, rut, rutling, pitman, pippermint, rutling, ribbling, nestlebird. It is obvious that these terms are rich and expressive because they are personal: they are terms of amused affection, and the loss to our language, once the richest in the world, lies precisely here, that it has become depersonalised, abstracted from nature. William Barnes, the Dorset poet, was so acutely conscious of this corruption that he would speak and write Saxon words only. If the average politician or banker or economist or publicist or "educationist" were compelled to write or speak in Saxon words only, should we not be immensely conscious of the poverty of their matter?

Much as I love William Barnes, I think he went a bit too far here. But if you look into the old English words of our wild flowers and bushes, whose sweetness and beauty are universally acknowledged, you will find that nearly all are Saxon words – coltsfoot, Whitsun bosses, henbane, bittersweet, primmy rose, eglantine, dewberry, codlins and cream, marigold etc. Even those that come from the Latin are completely anglicised and so native. The amazing thing is that a great number of our extremely English flower names bear the same meaning in old French (bittersweet – *douce amère*; coltsfoot – *pas d'âne*; goat's rue – *rue de chèvre*; devil's bit scabious – *mort du diable*, etc.) and I cannot imagine how this mysterious event took place.

H. J. MASSINGHAM

A CURE FOR WARTS
(1943)

Sir, A few days ago I met in Hertfordshire an elderly countryman who confided to me a sure cure for warts. Incidentally, the old man is the champion hedger and ditcher in the area in which he lives; a craftsman who would delight the heart of Mr. Massingham. You count the number of warts with which you are afflicted; you then cut on a bit of wood in the ground. By the time the piece of wood has rotted and has been absorbed into the soil the warts will have "dropped off". He had had two big 'uns on his hand which had been treated so successfully by this method that he recommended it with confidence.

His cure for influenza was rather more complicated and certainly much more expensive. A week come Tuesday he had felt badly and realised he was sickening for that there influenza. So he had knocked off at dinner time and visited the Crown on his way home. There he

*had two pints of Burton, fortified with two double rums (his
astonishment that I did not appreciate the difference between mere ale
and "Burton" was quite genuine, "seven and tuppence gorn in
twenty minutes and it never touched me." The expenditure was well
justified, however, as he felt grand the next morning. As a cure the
cost is not daunting, but I fear many of us less hardy individuals
might be "touched" to the extent of not being able to find the way
home from our own particular Crown.*

*There had not been much luck in rearing a large family and the
loss in particular of one of the elder children was an abiding grief.
"They do say as she died of the north wind: she 'ad 'ad the measles,
you see, and then she died of the north wind."*

*A fine old man: may he be spared for many a year to go on
dealing with his ailments with such outstanding success.*

R. LANGFORD JAMES

... MORE ABOUT NETTLES
(1860)

Growing on waste and neglected places, flourishing alike
on breezy commons and in the dirty ditches of the suburbs,
the nettle has neither beauty nor fragrance to recommend it
to the ordinary observer. Yet it is well worth careful
inspection on account of the beauty of its structure. True it
has a sting if handled gingerly, but seize the plant heartily and
it will give you little discomfort.

The nettle is a very common, low-bred, vulgar plant but,
nevertheless, in its family and alliances may be found some of
the noblest members of the vegetable kingdom: the bread-
fruit tree, the mulberry, the hop, the hemp, the fig, the
banyan and the deadly upas.

It has not been without its affectionate admirers, as the
following anecdote will testify: A worthy floriculturist (not a
native of the south of England) was showing his green-house
to some ladies, when one of them said to him, "What is that
in the flower-pot? It is very like a nettle." "Indeed, ma'am, it

is just a nettle; but it grew up so bonnily, puir thing, that I could na' think to pu' it." It is not for its botanical beauty or respectable connections that we wish to put in a word on behalf of the nettle, but for its uses. As an old-wife's remedy it is used in scurvy, gout, jaundice, hæmorrhage, paralysis, &c. Nettle-tea, as a spring drink, were it generally used, would frighten the proprietors of old Dr. Jacob Townshend's sarsaparilla. The stalks of the old nettle are little inferior to flax for making linen cloth and are used for that purpose in America, Siberia, Germany, and formerly in some parts of the British isles. The famous Indian grass-cloth, Chu-Ma, is woven from the fibres.

An excellent rennet is made from the nettle. The expressed juice makes a permanent green dye for wool. The root boiled with alum yields a good yellow dye. Dried and used as fodder, it is capital for cows, increasing the quantity and improving the quality of their milk. And one of the least of its virtues is that if fish be packed in it, it preserves the colour and bloom infinitely better than any other grass or umbrage, dried or green.

It is as a pot-herb that we would advocate its use, and the spring is the best time for gathering nettles for that purpose. To say that it is recommended by Loudon and Soyer is sufficient. It is said to resemble asparagus in flavour, but our experience would assimilate it with spinach.

And now, ye rich agricoles, if this weed is still unworthy of your notice, tell the poor to send their children to gather the nettles. They will prove a wholesome food and, as a spring diet, will be better relished by the little ones than the vernal brimstone and treacle.

W. A. R.

Sir, On reading the letter of your correspondent W. A. R. on the history and uses of the common nettle, I am induced to put in a word of warning respecting its indiscriminate adoption as an article of food. The first time I partook of it was in the spring of 1847, which I spent in North Wales. When I carried my treasure home I asked my land-lady to cook some for dinner, she strongly deprecated its use, saying, "It has made many people ill, sir: don't eat it." Contrary to her opinion, I persisted, and the result in a few hours was a severe attack of dysentery; on inquiry I found that some others in the village had suffered in a similar manner. Two years after, dining with a friend in Essex, he warmly recommended his spinach. I ate some, and in the night was attacked with dysentery. On meeting my friend next day he laughingly inquired how I enjoyed the nettles.

I would suggest to W. A. R. that the common nettle (Urtica dioica) is only used as a diuretic and antiscorbutic; it is the dead nettle (Urtica mortua) that is said to have influence in hæmorrhage, &c. In Yorkshire the common nettle is very generally eaten among the lower classes, and I think I have frequently traced attacks of dysentery and bowel complaint to its indiscriminate use as an article of food (but when made into beer I never heard of it producing any unpleasant results).

In conclusion, my experience would suggest the use of nettles to be contra-indicated in all persons where there is a tendency to irritation and relaxation of the bowels, and in those suffering from hæmorrhoids or constitutionally predisposed to this troublesome disease.

PERDIX

The white dead nettle (Lamium album), the purple hedge nettle (Lamium purpureum), and the common nettle (Urtica dioica) are all used medicinally. A strong decoction of the purple nettle is especially recommended in the very complaint which W. A. R. says the common nettle produces (dysentery). I have been told that the sting of the nettle is very like the poison fang of the rattlesnake.

FIREFLY

"Firefly" is quite correct when she draws a parallel between the fang of a poisonous reptile and the sting of a poisonous plant. The sting in poisonous plants, such as the nettle, consists of a delicately-elongated tube, which is seated upon a gland, in which the poisonous fluid is secreted, and when any pressure is made upon the gland the fluid passes into the tube. W. A. R. might be right: touch it gently and it will sting, but grasp it firmly and it harms not – it could be that the grasp breaks down the projecting hollow tube and the poison cannot therefore run along it, whereas the delicate touch allows the exceedingly sharp point of the tube to penetrate the skin and cause a wound.

F. T. BUCKLAND

(1958)

Sir, Having recently been stung by nettles, my thoughts went back to boyhood days in Wester Ross where the ancient cure for "the rheumatics" was to be beaten on the bare back by a switch of young nettles. Relatives of mine used to swear by the treatment. I have never heard of it elsewhere than in the Highlands. Perhaps no other race is hardy enough to undergo the treatment.

KENNETH MCLENNAN

THE HUMAN TOUCH
(1972)

Everybody has heard of gardeners for whom plants prosper to an unusual degree and who are said to have "green fingers"; most of us dismiss this pretty fancy as no more than a tribute to their experience and innate sympathy with their charges. But a Canadian horticulturist thought there might be more to it, and advanced the theory that the human hand might give off some chemical emanation which could affect the growth of plants either beneficially or adversely.

He looked for support and found it in the records of the Fisheries Research Board of Canada. Fishery officers were making a count of the salmon using the ladder on the Stamp River of Vancouver Island. Presently they saw a salmon marked with a tag making its way up and, wishing to learn its history, one of them waded barefoot into the line of pools to net it out. A moment later the run of fish stopped abruptly. The watchers were intrigued because the fish at the bottom of the ladder could certainly not have seen the man, and the roar of the falls close by precluded any possibility of sound or vibration having scared them. The only explanation seemed to be that wet skin had some repellent effect.

So they carried out tests and found it was necessary only to slide a hand gently into the water upstream of the fish to cause an instant drop in the number ascending the ladder. To give actual figures of the effect, when the rate of ascent was 30 fish every ten minutes the immersion of a hand caused a reduction to four salmon in the same time, and this was borne out in test after test.

Being interested, they experimented at other fish-ladders on other rivers and met the same effect. They then widened the scope of the tests and found that a basin of water in which clean hands had been soaked for one minute would not only stop a run temporarily but cause salmon to turn and swim downstream. Similar quantities of other liquids, ranging from sea-water to tomato-juice, went unheeded by the fish.

In the end, they had to conclude that the human skin gave off some smell or emanation that in the smallest quantities would stop a running fish in its tracks. The power of this emanation must be tremendous because the dilution was in the nature of one part in a hundred million which is roughly one drop in an Olympic swimming-pool. Not even the strongest garden chemicals are effective in such extreme dilution. So our horticulturist is continuing his researches into "green fingers" with the knowledge that the human skin can give off something of tremendous potency, though whether it affects plant-life is still unknown.

I told this true story to a well-known expert who earns a living advising market-gardeners how to improve their crops, and he capped it. He had been called in to help two brothers who were worried because they never grew a completely successful crop. Always a proportion of the plants would do poorly, yet there was no visible disease or pest to explain it.

He could not make head or tale of this happening for a long time until, to cut a long tale short, he suddenly found that the plants handled by one brother did well and those of the other were never robust. "It was fascinating," he said. "If the brother with the harmful touch wore rubber gloves, the lettuces he transplanted did well, but if he used his bare hands the results were substandard."

"What did you advise?" I asked. "It was easy," he answered. "I put the one with the unhappy touch on to the administrative side, accounts, bills, records, orders and the like, while his brother worked only with the crops. But if there was a crisis and both had to work in the garden, then the first one wore gloves at all times. They are now a very successful little firm which is expanding yearly."

Perhaps that is why so many women are good gardeners. Vanity makes them wear gloves to keep their hands presentable.

C. C. L. BROWNE

ACTION MAN HAS A DAY ON THE LAKE
(1972)

The sound of the outboard motor ripped through the peace of the place like a band-saw through softwood as the boat roared clear of the diminutive island and headed into the wind towards the dam. The man at the tiller was sheathed in black oilskin and rubber, inside which internal combustion seemed to have taken place. Smoke from his pipe seeped through the few exposed cracks and crannies around his face and under the shiny black sou'wester.

"Only sport that attracts me. Can't stand the competitive kind. Bit of peace and quiet's all I need. Everybody needs a bit of relaxation – specially after a week on the forecourt, flogging motor-cars. The old bronchials need a decoke; know what I mean?" He wore very thin Italian driving gloves – black leather – and polaroid glasses.

Only his nose, and the drip gathering on the end of it, gave the game away: this was a human being and not a life-sized Action Man. Coot and moorhen scattered as the boat hurled itself through the lumpy water, its fibreglass hull thumping, rowlocks shivering, seatboards clattering. The tips of six fishing rods quivered and chattered with the vibration of it all.

An almost identical figure in field green knelt on the juddering bottom boards. "Colin here, he's my top junior salesman. No recreations or hobbies at all – except the back row of the Odeon – till I got at him. Changed his whole attitude, a spot of quiet fishing." He raised his voice to carry over the engine din: "Colin!" The field-green figure looked up. "Yes, Mike!" he yelled back. The man at the tiller glanced at the sky, remembered his polaroid glasses, pushed them up, surveyed the sky again and then looked down at the water creaming away from the boat.

"First drift – ready? Right! Here's the order, then. Tapered line. Shooting head. Number Two rod – no, make it Number Three. Number Two's a bit weak. Top dropper – Thunder and Lightning. Dunkeld on the middle, and a special on the tail OK?" His companion nodded. "Colin – make the droppers a decent length this time, will you?" It was an order, not a request.

The field-green figure genuflected on the bottom boards and pulled out a square blue fibreglass box. Shielding it with his rubberized body from the flying spray, he swung it open. Three hinged trays tiered neatly below the lid, each tray divided into compartments, each compartment containing split shot, casts, flies, lures, hooks, in dazzling multiplicity.

"Neat, isn't it? American, natch. Can't be doing with little tin boxes and lumps of cork. The cork falls to bits, and you need fingernails like chisels to get 'em open. Had some good Perspex ones once, but they went overboard." He swung the boat round in a half-circle, coming up parallel with the dam and perilously close, and killed the out-board. The concrete

wall towered over the boat and clouds spun away over it.
Action Man pointed to the thick-fringed skirt of weed at the
bottom of the concrete cliff.

"They have a nibble at that, but the wind's wrong to have
a go at them there today." He bent forward and pulled a small
bundle of cloth and rope from under his seat. The nearest
boat was miles away, but he still glanced over his shoulder as
he dropped the furtive bundle over the side. It ballooned
instantly and parachuted down into the green water.

"Not really kosher, but in this wind you drift too fast.
Handy little sea-anchor. French, that one. Dries up in a
minute. If there's a sniff of a water bailiff, you can have it up,
squeezed out and in your pocket before he alters course.
Right, let's go!" He snapped his fingers and the butt of a rod
presented itself to his hand with operating theatre precision.

He whipped the rod tip quickly through the air a couple
of times, testing its balance, and then began to cast. The rod
was short and stubby with enormously springy action. The
reel squealed and his left hand fed out line.

At first it was only his wrist, moving in classic casting
style, then his forearm, then his whole shoulder, pumping
out a cast of incredible length. The line shot out as straight as
a wire, the flies hovered in immaculate formation over the
water, shot another 10 ft. as the weight of the shooting head
propelled them from behind, and dropped. Almost before the
first fly hit the water, Action Man began stripping the line in,
his left hand a blur.

"Used to go through a rod a week, fishing every day.
Smashed the tips. Split cane! I'll say! All right for old
gentlemen on piddling little streams, I suppose. Tried all the
best fishing-tackle shops up and down Piccadilly and St.
James's when I first decided to go in for trout." He cast again,
flailing the flies through the air, the line swinging like a
ringmaster's whip behind him. "Tried the orthodox rods?
Cost me a packet, I don't mind telling you. Didn't it Colin?"

The field-green figure was now belabouring the water in
similar manner, though slower. "Thought I'd have to chuck it
in, till I saw this little fibreglass job. Sea-fishing. Put two and
two together, found a little fellow down Acton way, and he

turns 'em out for me special. Lovely jobs." The rod dipped
and bent. "Ah! Here we go. First of the drift. Play 'em hard,
that's what I always say."

He reeled in hard, his line as taut as piano-wire. A
rainbow trout floundered towards the boat, just below the
surface, drowning with its mouth open. It was netted and
despatched with as much elegance as a mackerel on a summer
holiday fishing trip. Action Man felt in his belt for his fishing
scales, while Colin set to work with the gouger.

"Trouble is, with this method – when they're hooked,
they're hooked, by God!" The mutilated fish was weighed.
"Two-six," sang out Action Man and Colin chalked the
figures with a chinagraph pencil on a plastic jotting pad. "Bit
hard on the hands, though." He pulled off the thin black
leather gloves. The sticking plaster on his right index finger
was nearly cut through. Every finger had its bandage –
Jeremy Fisher bitten by a stickleback.

"Worth it, though. Get our limit in the morning, pop
them in the cold box in the boot of the car, drive down to
the mooring apron and wander in with a second lot after the
evening rise. Not that you get much rise on a lake like this.
Wind's dropped nicely now though. Colin! Slap a Hairy
Mary on the tail will you?" His cast was like a length of
barbed wire. Each of the three flies were triple-hooked,
enormous, vulgar, efficient.

"More like spinning?" He looked shocked. "Who says? It's
fly fishing, this is." He was indignant. "Scientific fly fishing,
that's all. You check your speed of drift, depth of fly, length of
cast, don't you? Well?" He was suddenly aggressive. "Spinning,
you just drag your lure through the water and hope for the
best. What's the score, Colin? Ten? It's not six o'clock yet.
Chuck those two little 'uns over the side and let's fish on."

The lake was suddenly calm as the sun dipped behind the
island. Midges and silver-wings began to dance. A boat,
unhampered by outboard or secret sea-anchor, glided lightly past.
In the stern, an elderly man in a tweed fishing hat and ancient
shooting jacket cast a perfect dry fly to the first rise of the evening.

"Hey!" shouted Action Man. "Watch where you're going!
You're crossing our drift!" The purist cast again, deaf and

blind to everything but the perfect presentation of dry fly on still water. "Aaaagh! Now that's a bit too much! Did you see that? Did you see him? Straight across our drift!"

He gunned the outboard suddenly, shouted to Colin to reel in, swung his boat in a tight circle round the perfectionist who had just regained his balance after the sudden shock of the engine noise and was staring with bewilderment at the cause of this outrageous breach of etiquette.

He looked like an old retriever who has blundered on to the side of a motorway. A group of mallard flurried into the air with football-rattle alarm cries, and coot and moorhen scooted for cover. Action Man sounded aggrieved: "You don't expect that sort of thing on a lake like this, do you? Know what I mean?" He paused.

"Christ, but my arm is stiff." He moved his shoulder sorely in its socket and wound a fresh piece of waterproof sticking plaster round his right index finger. "What's the score, Colin? Twelve? Ditch the two little 'uns and they'll average just under three apiece. Not bad, eh? What do we do with 'em? Give 'em away, sometimes. Freeze a few good-lookers. That one there – lovely deep fish, that one. The rest go to the local fish merchant.

"Can't abide the taste, myself. Prefer lobster. Fair exchange, eh?" Gold reflections from the setting sun rippled across the water. "Just time for a quick bit of plug-holing, eh, Colin?" The outboard whisked the gold ripples into foam. "Down by the dam," he explained. "Get some good fish there, sometimes, by the outlet. Not much sport, but you can kill a few. They get their noses down, half asleep, I reckon. Take anything you offer. What? Sell 'em?"

He sounded injured and incredulous. "Me? You don't do this sort of thing for profit, you know!" He paused. "It's a sport, isn't it?" The roar of the outboard drowned the quiet singing of an old reel as the purist played his first fish of the day as gently as a mother teaching her child to swim.

RACHAEL FEILD

BANSHEE
(1920)

He stood there, chained to wall and rack
With trebled steel. "For God's own sake,"
The scared groom croaked to me, "Stand back!
You never know — those chains might break!"

Within the dim light of the stall
I saw the wild eyes red with hate,
And marked the ten-year hatter-gall
That told the ceaseless strife with fate.

He heard a strange foot on the floor,
A strange voice in the shadows sound,
And strained his fetters with a roar
That shook the shed from roof to ground.

The foam upon his lips was white,
His bitten breast was flecked with cream;
He screamed — a soul in piteous plight —
Hate, fear, and anguish in the scream.

"Why keep him tortured, chained, and mad,
And dungeoned from the daylight's gold?"
"His blood's the best we ever had,
And all his stock are sound and bold."

Maybe ... I crossed the sunlit lanes
And only saw with eyes a-swim
The torn brown breast, the trebled chains,
The wild eyes in the twilight dim.

WILL H. OGILVIE

April

NEST BUILDING MATERIALS
(1969)

Sir, At Easter, in Harrow, I washed out a plastic flower pot and placed it on a coal bunker to dry off in the sun. Shortly afterwards a blackbird settled nearby, picked up the pot and flew off with it. Unfortunately it proved too heavy and the bird managed to fly only about four yards before dropping it on to the garden. It was a 4 ¹/₂ in. "half-pot" – roughly the size of a blackbird's nest. Are blackbirds turning to prefabricated nesting material?

G. ORME

(1942)

Sir, I wonder if you have any record of barbed wire being used as nesting material? Such was the unusual choice of a kite (now deceased), which had selected an electric pylon as its temporary home.

The consumers of this particular commodity were made widely aware of the bird's presence by a series of blinding flashes and a failure in the electric supply. Engineers removed the offending nest but within a few hours the bird was busy again with its barbed wire entanglements.

The only method of restoring the situation was the "liquidation" of the culprit, and the bird was dispatched at dawn the next day.

S. P. O. D. EIPPING

SEEKING COMPANY
(1959)

Once I suggested that we might well be breeding in these overcrowded islands a race of human beings of which only a few individuals could endure solitude except for a very brief spell. All the rest needed their daily dram of noise and talk and crowds and bustle before they regarded themselves as living at all. That suggestion brought, queerly enough, letters from all over the world, and from very varied correspondents, who were scattered from London to Kuala Lumpur, from East Anglia to Abadan. All they wanted was a chance to live in seclusion, and be on their own, and earn a modest living while doing so. Whether all of them could endure genuine loneliness for more than a few months is one of those things which only a boggle of psychologists could predict, and they are, men say, occasionally wrong. Several of my correspondents clearly needed, like so many of us, solitudes which were not in the tropics or the Persian Gulf or Auskerry, but within a cannon shot of civilisation.

But it is disconcerting to realise that many birds are apparently as much in need of companionship as we are and that solitude, even in their honeymoon seasons, does not appeal to them. I am writing this in a part of the Highlands which shall be nameless, at almost the end of a glen which is as lovely as it is inaccessible. For 20 or 30 square miles the human population must be as low as anywhere in these islands. Hikers are far between. You would expect hundreds of birds to throng to that area in the breeding season, seeking in May the seclusion from disturbance which a human being would consider to be their first requirement after food.

Yet with the possible exception of the three real mountain aristocrats, the golden eagle, the ptarmigan and the dotterel, all of whom pay a high price in bleakness and cold and slashing rain for their seclusion, you would find 90 per cent of the birds in this vast area within a mile, sometimes within 200 yards of a croft or the house of a stalker or a shepherd.

The farther you climb into the remoteness all around, which stretches ever wider and steeper before you, the fewer the birds. You will never waste your time there, unless you are one of those beings who gets bored with absolute silence and the grandeur of distance and the circle of snow-slashed hills which are an enchantment in themselves. But you will not see many birds there, and your field glasses will hardly be needed except to look at deer. Yet in a week as hot as mid-July I have watched, within 300 yards of a shepherd's house, 23 species of birds almost jostling one another along the edge of the loch, and four other species within a short mile. And that is very nearly the lot.

Exactly the same phenomenon of how birds dislike solitude can be seen elsewhere. There are virgin hill forests in northern Burma, where no man goes off the path and where if you try uphill or down, however patiently you sit and watch, you will see and hear no bird. In Swedish Lapland, likewise, I once selected from the map an area of bog and lake, tundra and woodland to explore in June which was as secluded as it looked enticing. Surely, I thought, this is where the birds will be and I shall not be disturbed in watching them. But when I had tramped over 20 miles that day and seen almost nothing, my companions, who shunned walking and had been sight-seeing to Narvik by train, smiled at me patronisingly. Next day they took me to a railway station where on a rood of fetid pond, flanked by a factory and locomotives in need of water, was a concentration of breeding birds, stints, phalaropes, redshanks, duck, and a reeve, such as one might go far to encounter. Similarly you will watch more wild duck in St. James's Park than you will see on remote waters where man is only occasional.

What the explanation is I do not know. It is certainly not that the presence of many gives birds extra security. I saw a large gullery in the Great Glen, within 20 yards of a main road and so near a large camp of hydro-electric workers that it seemed doomed to be despoiled. It is certainly not a question of the food supply, for I am quite sure that in the summer quite adequate food is found over a great area which is never colonised. There is nothing geographical about it. Is it perhaps that one species attracts another by its very presence, as human crowds are formed from a sense of companionship? There is a small gullery near here, just two pairs of common gulls, each of which has an oyster catcher sitting on eggs within a few yards of them. Is it that any commotion and disturbance attracts a crowd of birds, as people flock curiously to an accident or follow a marching procession?

I do not know. All I know is that I have walked miles of empty hill and glen and in the matter of birds I have gone farther and fared worse, though there are no blank days in the hills in May. But if I had never left the lodge I should have seen far more, a medley of greenshank and widgeon, an old duck mallard with her young, then a redshank, then a common sandpiper, then perhaps a lesser black-black or a black-headed gull, with other ducks as well. The shallows in which they parade and feed are as public and as crowded as the Ritz. Perhaps they come to stare, to see how other birds eat, or what new plumage they are wearing. Birds may possibly flock to such places out of mere curiosity, as we do. Dare I suggest, with Mr. James Fisher in the offing, that the southward spread of the fulmar is due, not to the plankton, but to the fact that its human admirers have left St. Kilda?

J. K. Stanford

HOW AND WHEN BIRDS SLEEP
(1943)

Sir, – Recent letters to The Field have touched on a topic to which I feel I might add a little information. I am in agreement with your correspondent who says, "It would be a good test of one's knowledge of birds to be able to say where they slept." I got my knowledge of birds' sleeping habits mostly from the pursuit of a somewhat barbarous method of destroying the too numerous and mischievous ones, that is, by searching them out with a powerful light and shooting them with an air rifle. Sparrows were the most sought quarry, and while looking for them hundreds of other species were

observed, notably the greenfinch, chaffinch, robin, bullfinch and
blackbird. Of course, we never thought of harming such birds as
these, for when picked up in the beam of the light they were instantly
recognised and left to their peaceful dreams.

I give a list of birds and their usual roosting places; they do roost in
other places, but they mostly select their own peculiar spots, if available.

Common house sparrow. – Very seldom away from human
habitations, never in the open hedgerow, usually on ledges under
sheds, under the eaves of houses, in thick ivy on house walls, in old
martins' nests and under the eaves of a thatched rick.

Greenfinch. – Always in bunches or flocks, in holly trees or thick
ivy stumps on the leeward side, sometimes in company with a few
chaffinches, but very seldom, nearly always alone, never in buildings
or under eaves.

Blackbird. – In rather open exposed places, a good rough
blackthorn or bramble bush, never more than six feet up, sometimes a
laurel bush, always a solitary sleeper, and always very wide awake.

Missel-thrush. – Another lone sleeper, usually high up, close
against the trunk of some tree, usually an ivy clad tree.

Song-thrush. – Holly bunches, garden shrubs, etc.

Robin. – Always low down, not too sheltered and never under
buildings, any small shrub or low hedge, even amongst the finches in
a holly tree, nearly always with his head tucked closely over the back
and under the wing feathers.

Wren. – Most often in an old wren's nest, nearly always in
bunches (I have counted 11 coming out of one old moss nest),
sometimes in holes in old thatch or holes in trees.

Blue-tit. – Like the wren, perhaps for warmth they get together
in threes and fours tightly huddled up in some hole in a thatched roof
or tree or crack in a wall, never in the open hedgerow.

Linnets. – Favour wild places, heaths and hill-tops where gorse
and thick yew trees abound, favour yew, and sometimes tall bracken.

Yellow-hammer. – Low down in thick hedges, very often on the
ground, in the open field, especially grassland.

Bullfinch. – Always alone in the barest hedgerow, the more
spikes and thorns the better.

Jay. – In small bunches on the edge of a wood, low down in some
tree that holds a few dead leaves, a holly tree in the wood, or perhaps
some other evergreen.

Woodpigeon. – In vast companies, in fir plantations and open beech woods.

Sparrow-hawk. – In tall trees, beech, oak or, if available, some solitary pine, often in company with pigeons.

Starling. – In vast flocks at specially favoured spots, laurel plantations, big shrubberies and reed beds.

These are only a few of the many birds I have seen roosting, and perhaps in other parts of the country the same species select different locations for sleep; but you will have noticed, I think, that the birds I have mentioned mostly select their roosting quarters in very much the same surroundings as they select their nesting sites; in fact, so similar, I think, that if you wish to see a certain species roosting look for it where you would normally seek its nest; it will not be very far away.

Douglas England

Sir, – In a recent issue, Mr. W. W. Nicholas stated: "It would seem that when a curlew is truly asleep, the head is buried behind the wing." I am able to add, through personal observation, that this is also the case in two of our smaller birds; though when incubating eggs, they sometimes appear to go into a form of sleep, which perhaps might be termed boredom.

In June of this year I had a robin's nest under observation, which contained six eggs. One day when the robin had been incubating for five days I visited the nest at noon and found her with her head drooping over the side of the nest facing me, and her eyes closed; I placed my finger near her to see what the reaction would be. The robin literally shook herself and then darted at my fingers, swerving just as it appeared she would hit them. The usual alarm note was then uttered a few yards away.

As I was not certain whether this was the way a robin usually slept, I returned the same night after dark and with the aid of a torch discerned that she had her beak and head tucked behind one of her wings, the body feathers were fluffed out, and the bird appeared fast asleep. I did not disturb her further.

The previous spring I had a similar experience with a tree-creeper, only during her daytime sleep, owing to the confined space, the head was held up against the wood which enclosed the true nest. If the *form of sleep which is taken during the daytime is not as I suggest – boredom – is there any biological reason why the two methods of nesting should take different forms? Or might a simile be drawn between an afternoon sleep in an armchair without undressing and the normal procedure of changing into night attire and pulling the bedclothes over oneself?*

P. A. ADOLPH

FLOWER RECIPES
(1934)

A French lady once told me that the juice of strawberries was a good thing for removing freckles; also violets boiled in goat's milk – Theodosia. (1860)

Most folk associate flower recipes with old vellum-bound volumes and the recipes therein contained as being of purely antiquarian interest. It is true that the vast majority of the recipes, or "receipts" as our ancestors usually spelt it, are far too complicated for these hurried days, and it must be acknowledged that some of the gems would be of no value in these over-civilised times. For instance, the ninth-century antidote for one poisoned by his step-mother – a decoction of horehound. Many of the recipes, however, are simple and practical, and for the last twenty years or so I have collected them from many sources – both from people and books. I am confining this article to a few recipes for spring flowers with no reference to those that were of medicinal interest, nor to wines.

Amongst spring flowers few were more commonly used than cowslips. The flowers and leaves were a common ingredient in salads; cowslip creams and puddings, tea and syrup, cowslip candy and pickle, to say nothing of complexion washes, were made in most households.

Cowslip cream is a confection fit for Titania. It is made by mixing a little cowslip syrup with cream, thickening the cream with whites of eggs beaten to a froth, adding candied cowslips and garnishing also with candied cowslips. Cowslip syrup is made by infusing 3 lb. of fresh cowslip flowers in two quarts of boiling water and leaving it till quite cold and then simmering to a syrup with sugar, allowing a pound of sugar to a pint of water. Candying cowslips is very easily done; the freshly-gathered clusters should be dipped in a solution of gum arabic, gently shaken in a cloth and then powdered thickly with the finest sifted sugar and hung on a string to dry near the fire. They should be left to dry three days and then packed in layers in air-tight boxes. Mrs. Mary Eales, who was confectioner to Queen Anne, gives the recipe, but says nothing about storing the flowers.

John Evelyn, in Actuarial, gives a recipe for pickled cowslips, made by pouring a pint of boiling white wine vinegar in which a pound of white sugar has been dissolved over a pound of cowslip flowers. Cowslip pudding is not for these thrifty days, for it requires eight eggs to a pint and a half of cream. It is made by mixing half a gallon of cowslip flowers, chopped finely, with Madeira cake rubbed to crumbs and incorporating the whole with a pint and a half of cream, thickened with the yolks and whites, beaten separately, of eight eggs and served in an open tart garnished with cowslips.

For cowslip complexion lotion, simmer half a peck of cowslip blossoms in a wide, shallow pan. The flowers should be first covered with cold water, brought slowly to the boil and then simmered for an hour. Two large cucumbers are then finely sliced and added, and the water brought to the boil again for five minutes. Strain through clean muslin and when quite cold pour into bottles and tie down. This was one of the most commonly used complexion lotions in Victorian times.

Elder flower cream was made for sunburn, for softening the skin and for chilblains. I have frequently made this cream, which keeps good for quite two years, and I am very popular with my friends when I give them pots of it. Making it is very simple, but it takes time. Two pounds of the best fresh lard are put into a large bowl which is partly immersed in a saucepan of boiling water. When the lard is melted, 2 lb. of elder flowers are added, and the bowl is left over the saucepan all day, the fat being stirred every half-hour or so with a wooden spoon. The water in the saucepan must be frequently replenished. Then the fat is strained through clean muslin into little pots and when quite cold tied down. The fat smells very strongly of elder flowers and is quite pleasant to use.

Elder vinegar is useful as a change from ordinary vinegar. It is made by filling a jar half full of elder flowers, not too tightly packed, and filling up with boiling white wine vinegar.

The humble coltsfoot is despised nowadays, but was once so highly esteemed that formally the apothecaries of Paris used to paint a coltsfoot on the doorposts. Syrup of coltsfoot has a very attractive taste. It is made by pouring a quart of water over 1/2 lb. of coltsfoot flowers three times, i.e. when the first infusion is cold it is strained and the water poured over a fresh 1/2 lb. of the flowers. When cold, the third infusion is boiled to a syrup with 2 lb. of white sugar.

Violets were used almost as many ways as cowslips. The young leaves were not only used for salads, but also fried in batter and eaten with lemon or orange juice. John Evelyn describes violet leaves served thus as "one of the most agreeable of all the herbaceous dishes." Violet milk, made by steeping violets in milk, was highly esteemed as a complexion wash. Violet vinegar is made in the same way as elder vinegar, while violet tablet is a delicious sweet. This is made by steeping violet flowers in the juice and a pound of sugar and boiling to candy height. When nearly cold is it cut into squares.

Violet syrup is made by steeping 2 lb. of fresh violets in five pints of water for 24 hours. Then strain off the flowers and add sugar to the liquor, allowing a pound of sugar to each pint of water and boil to a syrup. In olden days housewives were very particular to use soft water, and I have found that if hard water is used the results are not so satisfactory.

Eleanour Sinclair Rohde

Will "Theodora" be so good as to say if the violets and goat's milk should be prepared fresh daily, and how it should be used; whether the face should be washed at night or in the morning; also if the juice of strawberry jam would answer, or should it be the juice of fresh-gathered strawberries? – Nannie (1860)

UMBRELLA FOR THE ROOSTERS ...
(1965)

It is a poor hen that cannot find one grain of corn in a farmyard and so, when a visitor said that she had just solved the problem of how to decoy roosting chickens down out of a tree, I pricked up my ears even though the answer seemed likely to be of scant use to me. "Sometimes I'm late putting them to bed," she explained, "and I find them twenty feet up on a branch. I suppose they'd be all right there but I do like them to be shut up at night. What would you do?" I answered that my free-winged guinea-fowl are left to their own devices and that, short of shinning up the tree and scragging them, I had no solution to offer.

"You stand under their branch," she went on, "with a black umbrella, and you suddenly open it over your head." It seemed to me a wise precaution but I only asked what reaction the birds showed. "They fall straight out of the tree and, provided you close your umbrella again quickly, they cluster round you for protection and follow you to wherever you want to take them. They must think the umbrella is a huge crow."

I was becoming a little dizzy but I did not think she was pulling my leg, so this evening as dusk fell, I took my brolly for a walk to the walnut-tree, feeling as ill-dressed as if I were attending a wedding reception carrying an ice-axe. The four were thirty feet up, and as I approached they craned downwards, muttering mutinously to each other. I placed myself where I would not be in the impact centre should it suddenly come on to rain guinea-fowl and then opened my gamp with aplomb.

Nothing stirred, so I peered up. Each bird was staring straight ahead of it, registering the well-bred disgust of aristos in a tumbril for the canaille around, and I crept away abashed for they were clearly not going to descend to my level.

Before I shut up the penned ones, I tried unfurling my brolly at them, but except for a skip in the air and a squawk or two they were neither intrigued nor dismayed. So I offer this valuable poultry tip with reservations. It may, of course, be that, living at the foot of a rookery, they care not a snap of the beak for large, black birds, and that in a normal setting the stratagem will pay off. But I am not interested because life is short, and if my flock like to roost up aloft out of each of foxes I am not going to waste time trying to sheepdog them down.

C. C. L. Browne

... AND HOW TO GET YOUR OWN
(1860)

There is no need of stealing an umbrella – they can be got without. Take your stand in a doorway on a rainy morning. When you see a man coming along with a nice silk article, step out and say to him, "Sir, I beg your pardon, you have my umbrella." In nine cases out of ten he will instantly surrender it. How does he know it was not you he stole it from?

An American

THE ORIGIN OF JORROCKS
(1934)

Sir, I heard my father, the late Major E. N. Heygate, R.E., of Buckling, Leominster, tell the following story on various occasions. For over ten years he was on the Ordnance Survey of Co. Durham, and was generally quartered at Darlington.

Being a keen hunting man, he found time to get a good bit of hunting, and it was when out with the Hurworth that he first met Mr. Surtees. Mr. Surtees was a peculiar man – very reserved, scarcely spoke to anyone, scarcely answered when addressed. Consequently people got in the habit of chaffing him – questioning him in order to draw him. On one occasion, being perhaps rather more hunted than usual, he suddenly burst out: *"I will bet any man fifty sovereigns that within one year from this day I will write a book that will make all England laugh."*

Three or four men at once took up the bet, my father amongst them, but Mr. Surtees declined more than the one £50 bet.

Time went on and the book appeared, and everyone read it, and was genuinely astonished.

Within the year at a meet of the hounds, the Master proposed a resolution, and someone seconded it, *"That in the opinion of this Hunt Mr. Surtees has won his bet."*

The resolution was carried with acclamation, and Mr. Surtees was paid his £50. Mr. Surtees certainly turned the tables on his critics.

W. B. HEYGATE

AN IBEX HUNT IN SUSSEX
(1901)

During one of the battles which annually take place in October amongst the herd of ibex inclosed in the beautiful park at Leonardslee, a certain billy received such a thrashing from the chief of the harem that he decided to leave the place. Accordingly, with a jump and a scramble, he was up and over the 7 ft. inclosure. He had decided to roam the wide world, and establish a colony of his own.

For some months nothing was heard of his movements, until he was found to be frequenting some coverts on the southern slope of Hurst Hill where one day in February he was seen by a keen sportsman, Dr. Juckes of Horsham, who, whilst driving along the high road was astonished to see a small dog rushing in wild panic from a neighbouring covert, closely pursued by an immense billy goat with a beard like a Free State Boer. Shortly afterwards he came to tell me about it, and we decided that it would be rather good sport to attempt the capture of the wild beast, which it was easy to recognise as the escaped ibex.

Sir Edmund Loder said that he would like to see his runaway captured, and Mr. Oliver having kindly given the doctor and myself permission to scour the country where the goat was residing, we began to make plans for the capture. The first thing to do was to "harbour" our quarry. This I managed to do without any difficulty, as for two months he had been living in a long strip of covert on the sloping hillside between the villages of Faygate and Rusper. Here the goat had exercised all the cunning of his race, for he only came out to feed in the grass fields at dawn and sunset, and had only twice been actually seen by Mr. Oliver's keeper, on whose ground his retreat was situated.

A meet was accordingly fixed at Mr. Campion's house on the morning of March 6, and there five keen sportsmen assembled, including Mr. B. Hall, a gentleman who had learnt to throw a lasso in the plains of the wild and woolly west, and we relied upon him to take Mr. Billy when brought to bay. At this rendezvous punctually arrived Mr. Child and five and a half couples of useful-looking hounds, who had the reputation of being willing to hunt anything from a red herring to an elephant. I confess that I never expected that we should have anything in the nature of a run, for there was every probability that our quarry would stand at once and fight the hounds, and thus be speedily captured; so that after the preliminary posting of horsemen it was somewhat of a surprise to find that the ibex, whom the hounds started almost immediately, had broken away to the west so silently and so swiftly that none of the field or the stray onlookers had seen him go. Subsequent events, however, proved that in his first rush to the west along through Hurst Hill Woods to Holbrook the ibex had gone at such a tearing gallop that he had run clean away from the two hounds that at first stuck to him. Here the goat struck the branch road which skirts Mrs. Creyke's park, and running at a full gallop for half a mile in the direction of Horsham, he turned west again towards Warnham Station, to which the field some five minutes behind followed him, guided only by the heavy spoor on the soft road.

At last, down by Chennel's Brook, we came on a gipsy boy who had not only viewed the object of our pursuit, but had seen him jump on to the bridge and drop 12 ft. in the field the other side, an altogether impossible leap for a horse.

Now things began to get exciting. Nearly everyone we passed had seen the goat. We galloped past my house, where the old ruffian seemed to have held us in such contempt that he amused himself for a minute or two, like some caprine De Wet, by jumping twice backwards and forwards over the great eight-barred gates of the Horsham and Three Bridges line, a piece of pardonable diversion from our point of view, since it enabled us to gain considerably upon him.

However, as we left the village behind and again entered the open country, several serious obstacles presented themselves in the shape of some really big fences, banks and ditches, and I was quite thankful when four or five of these had been overcome and I was still beside my friends, for I am not a regular hunting man, and cannot understand that stupid system of cutting off a horse's mane, when nature obviously intended that it should be placed there for man's support and assistance in time of trouble.

We were now heading again towards the hills, and, as the last view holloa had seemed more than usually near, I decided to cross a small strip of covert to the other side to obtain a better view. It was a lucky thought, for as Mr. Alec Lyon and I jumped out, the ibex, with two hounds at his stern, burst from the covert within fifty yards.

It was a really fine sight: the hounds ran almost mute, and at intervals the goat stopped and made a slash with his horns at his nearest pursuer. He was, however, now getting a bit tired, and soon we had the goat at bay in a corner of a field where there was a deep pit covered with undergrowth and willow saplings. Into this he at once jumped when he saw Mr. Hall swinging his lasso, and though that gentleman pursued him cautiously into his retreat he could not manipulate the lasso owing to the thickness of the covert. We were really rather pleased when the quarry once again made off over the open country, as there was some fear of his being torn by the hounds in such a close corner.

The closing scene was now at hand, for at the end of a long run, combined with excitement and savage worritings, even the strength and resource of an ibex will flag: so we soon had him up in a corner, where Mr. Hall easily threw the rope over him. Even then the gallant beast would not give in, but started off across the fields again. It was a last effort, however. The man of ropes knew how to stop and throw a running steer, but with his untutored English horse he got no purchase, though he did make the goat stand, when, someone kindly holding my horse, I got hold of his horns, threw the now tired beast and tied his legs.

It is not every day that we have an opportunity of chasing a ruminating animal like that of an ibex, and that he should have given a good hunting run of nine or ten miles as fast as stag or fox was certainly surprising.

J. G. MILLAIS

BELZUNG'S PATENT BOTTLE
(1853)

This is a very neat and simple little invention, which has for its object to substitute for corks a more convenient and equally secure method of closing bottles. For years the thing has been attempted, but unsuccessfully. Now, however, a machine has been patented which makes the thread of a screw outside the neck of a bottle when manufactured, without any loss of time, any increase of labour, or any extra

expense. The caps fitted on this screw may be made of gutta
percha, copper, tin, zinc, and all alloys. It is quite unnecessary
to point out the advantages of the invention.

ANON.

TO A WORM
(1935)

Puir hummle worm!
Ye creenge, an' crawl,
An' twist, an' turn.

In sike an' seuk, wi'oot a sound,
Ye tak' your pleesures underground.
Ye've neither eyes, nor lugs, nor wings:
Was ever born sic' hummle things?

Ye turn the earth whiles fowk ha'e sleep,
An' drain the bogs, when ye gae deep;
Ye pu' doon leaves tae mak' your food.
Lash! let us hope they dae ye guid.

'Mang men, the anglers lo'e ye weel -
Forbye they prog your heart wi' steel.
Tae hae heuks whammeled through your wame
Maun gar ye awfu' jigs o' pain.

They say ye dinna need a wife -
Nae muckle joy's in your short life.
Ye daft-like, dowdie, spineless thing,
Ye canna' even boast a sting.
An' sae, puir worm!
Ye creenge, an' crawl,
An' twist, an' turn.
Nae wonner!

PERCY MAIL

WALKING IS GOOD
(1853)

Walking is good: not stepping from shop to shop, or from neighbour to neighbour, but stretching out far into the country to the freshest fields, and highest ridges, and quietest lanes. However sullen the imagination may have been among its griefs at home, here it cheers up and smiles. However listless the limbs may have been when sustaining a too heavy heart, here they are braced, and the lagging gait becomes buoyant again.

However perverse the memory may have been in presenting all that was agonising, and insisting only on what cannot be retrieved, here it is first disregarded, and then it sleeps. The mere breathing of the cool wind on the face in the commonest highway is rest and comfort. The fields are better still, for there is the lark to fill up the hours with mirthful music, or, at worst, the robin and the flocks of fieldfares, to show that the hardest day has its life and hilarity. But the calmest region is the upland, where human life is spread out beneath the bodily eye, where the eye moves from the pheasant's nest to the spiry town, from the school-house to the churchyard, from the diminished team in the patch of fallow, or the fisherman's boat in the cove, to the viaduct that spans the valley, or the fleet that glides, ghost-like on the horizon. This is the perch where the spirit plumes its ruffled and drooping wings, and makes ready to let itself down any wind that heaven may send.

Miss Martineau

71

AUTOMOBILISM AND RESPIRATORY AILMENTS
(1902)

The appeal made by Dr Léon-Petit to the members of the Touring Club de France for detailed information as to the effect of automobilism on respiratory diseases has produced an abundant yield of answers. Two letters, both from physicians, are of peculiar interest as indicating different, but not irreconcilable views. One states that he has anticipated the benefits of automobilism by subjecting such patients as suffer from consumption, asthma and bronchitis to a strong current of air, such as would be experienced in driving a car at the rate of 120 kilometres an hour.

The patient first sits at some distance from the point of entrance of the hurricane, and gradually approaches till he can endure its full blast, much as one gradually acclimatises oneself to the successive temperatures in the rooms of a turkish bath. By these means the physician claims to secure all the advantages of swift automobilism without the disadvantages of nervous strain, which he considers to undo much of the good otherwise attained, of policemen and, no doubt, of dust and exposure to the chances of weather.

Another doctor, himself a sufferer from consumption, found marked benefit from a single automobile ride, during which his chronic cough temporarily left him. This he believes to be due to the rapid vibration which has a most beneficial effect on the system. The chief drawbacks to the automobile cure he considers to be the risk of exposure to rain and damp and the dust, against which he wishes to make a crusade. The curative effects of a residence on the south coast of France he found to be counteracted by the dust arising from the incessant procession of automobiles, bicycles, and carriages. Therefore the automobilist should look for relief in quiet lanes rather than on crowded highways.

A professor of the Paris Faculty of Medicine has found great benefit to his nerves from the rush of air and *la trépidation rhythmée* of the automobile, while a surgeon, on the contrary, has observed a chronic stupefaction arising from the same vibration, which disappeared with the temporary abandonment of the sport.

Finally, a provincial doctor testifies to the beneficial effect of automobilism on his rheumatism, or rather uræmia, which seriously affected his digestion. Relief which other remedies had failed to afford was most marked, and his bulk was greatly reduced. If this latter statement be generally true, the chief taunt of the bicyclist against the automobilist will be robbed of its sting.

Aeacus

HORSESHOES
(1940)

From the earliest times, it seems, ways and means of preventing horses' hoofs from breaking have exercised men's minds. The ancient Greeks and Romans endeavoured to protect the hoofs of their draught animals with a kind of slipper or boot, which were fastened round the hoof, something in the manner of the lawn shoes used by the pony drawing the mower in modern times.

It is recorded that Nero had a chariot drawn by mules with shoes of silver and his wife Poppaea had her team shod in gold; and some early Asiatic peoples were in the habit of covering their horses' hoofs with leather or rope shoes to assist in getting over snow. Travellers in comparatively recent times have told us that in Japan it was the custom to protect hoofs with straw bound round; but it was not until the nineteenth century that iron nailed-on shoes were introduced there.

It is said that nailed plates were known as far back as the second century BC, but there does not seem much mention of them till the ninth century and they did not become general till the Middle Ages. It seems that shoeing became the practice as the paving of streets and the making of gravel roads extended.

Many history books claim that William the Conqueror introduced the shoeing of horses into England. He brought farriers with his army; he gave the city of Nottingham as a fief to one of his followers in part payment for shoeing the King's horses. Henry de Ferres or Ferrers who came over with William ostensibly got his surname from his job as inspector of farriers. His descendants bore six horseshoes as part of their arms.

But shoeing was known before then, as is clear from the fact that Welbeck in Nottinghamshire was held before the Conquest by a Saxon tenant by the service of "shoeing the King's palfrey on all four feet with the King's nails" as often as he should visit his Manor of Mansfield. If by chance he lamed the palfrey in the process, he was to substitute another of equal quality. Examples of Saxon horseshoes have been found in burial mounds in Berkshire.

The Domesday Book has many references to smiths, and six in the city of Hereford had their forges at the rent of a penny, in consideration of being liable to be called on to shoe the King's horses. Old shoes, more in the form of a plate covering much of the hoof, are often ploughed up in different parts of England. The farmers generally call them "Roman shoes" but it is more likely they are mediæval. I possess several of these, and they differ from one dug up in accredited Roman remains. The latter is very thickly coated with rust, but seems to be more in the form of a modern shoe.

From very early times the shoe seems to have been regarded as an amulet or charm against bad luck. It was used in this way by Christians, Jews, Turks and other peoples. The antiquarian Elworthy records that he had seen them for the purpose on buildings in Constantinople, Spain, Italy, Sicily and Egypt. In Holland a special virtue was supposed to be attached to a stolen specimen.

There was a long controversy in European countries as to whether shoes used as amulets should be in threes, fives or sevens; and whether the triangle, so formed, should have its apex above or below. The majority of people use one shoe only and favour it so placed that "the luck will not run out." But a well-known forge at Cromwell on the Great North

Road has brickwork in the form of a shoe, with its points to the ground, built around the entrance.

In Lincolnshire it was formerly the practice for farm workers to hang a polished shoe over the mantelpiece. It was said to bring good luck, and people of all classes seem to like horseshoes about – if not actually in the dwelling house, then on some outbuilding. John Aubrey records one in the porch

of a Sussex church to keep away witches, and he was told the practice was common. West country folks hung up such shoes or holed flints over the cowhouse door to keep away the pixies or fairies.

The cast shoe was valued as a special charm. It took on the very ancient qualities attributed to the crescent. There are some who make fun of these things, but Nelson nailed a horseshoe to the Mast of the *Victory*. Probably the most historic collection of horseshoes is at Oakham Castle, Rutlandshire. Up to the time of the Conquest the Manor of Oakham had been held by Edward the Confessor's wife and Westminster Abbey. William the Conqueror divided it between the Abbey and Henry de Ferrers. In the reign of Henry II, Walkelin de Ferrers built a fortified manor house, all of which remains is the Banqueting Hall, most famous for the unique collection of horseshoes nailed on its walls. The collection apparently originated from the right of the Lord of the Manor to demand a shoe from every person visiting his lordship for the first time. Many are of enormous size and highly decorated. Queen Elizabeth gave a magnificent specimen and there are a great many others well worth viewing.

As the old countrymen used to say: "May the horseshoe never be pulled from your threshold."

LIEUTENANT-COLONEL W. L. JULYAN

Sir, In the article "Horseshoes at Oakham Castle" I notice that the horseshoes are nearly all hanging downwards. Please inform me which way a horseshoe should be hung up. Most people say upwards, to keep the luck in. As a youngster, 1866 vintage, I seem to remember downwards.

EDWARD RICHARDSON

Sir, You say that downwards is the correct way for horseshoes to hang. I was under the impression that it was upwards, and this is confirmed by a friend in lines he wrote when sending a horseshoe to a friend on her birthday as follows:

St. Dunstan drove the devil away
with lucky horse's shoe;
May the same symbol keep at bay
All devils that trouble you.
Just hang it up above your door
With points upturned to heaven,
And catch the gleams that friends will pour
Your birthday joys to leaven.

A. L. S.

HENDIADYS AND HERBS
(1972)

The other day I came on the word "hendiadys," which conveyed nothing whatsoever to me, so I turned it up in the dictionary and learned that it meant "expression of a complex idea by two words coupled with "and." It seemed a lot of fuss and feathers about not much, but I expect the brothers Fowler, who constructed my dictionary, had the thing well buttoned-up and I am content to accept their definition as it stands.

But when later I had occasion to look up the word "herb" I was less easily satisfied because the two descriptions offered seemed anything but taut. The first one was "a plant whose stem is soft and dies down to the ground after flowering" and that would seem to cover such things as potatoes. The other definition was "a plant whose leaves etcetera are used for food, scent, medicine etcetera" and into this class would appear to fall such growths as cabbages, tobacco and even strawberries. It all seemed very vague and I fell back on Kipling's

> *"Anything green that grew out of the mould*
> *Was a wonderful herb to our fathers of old."*

It was not my ancestors who had me focusing on herbs but a descendant, for my youngest daughter had blarneyed me into helping her make a herb garden. She had it all doped out. It must be a plot on a south slope near to the kitchen, and she had chosen her ideal site and now wanted my help in breaking up the ground.

I sighed as I looked the location over. Eighty years ago it was covered by pigsties, and when once I had tried to rotovate it the machine met such rubble that it proceeded in a series of standing bucks. But my young herbalist was adamant, so I sighed again and set about the area with a pick. For only one thing do I claim credit. I managed to reduce the area to be picked over from the size of a tennis court to about 10 ft. by 3 ft. on the grounds that any greater width would prohibit the reaching of the crops in the centre.

It was hard digging. The weedy turf had to be torn up and thrown away and the rubble raked out or picked up by hand. And when that was done, my herbalist decreed that the soil was too heavy and I had to mix in a barrow-load of sand, and when that had been faithfully done the result looked too light and I had to add a load of manure, stirring, as Mrs Beaton would say, "to a creamy consistency".

As I laboured and larded the lean earth, my slave-driver told me how parsley makes horses mettlesome and that if you rub it on your hands vigorously and then draw a finger across a window the pane will break (though she added that this was hearsay). She also said that basil is a sacred plant of the Hindu gods, that you put borage in claret (it must be sub-standard if it benefits from having weeds thrust into it) and other curious gems of information. It all sounded pretty fair malarkey to me, but I conceded that she had done her herbal homework well. And so the long day wore on.

Only two points did I stress. There must be no caraway lest it appear on our tea-table in the loathsome form of seed-cake, and that I disliked the smell of marigolds and would prefer it to be a forgotten herb so far as we were concerned.

The garden is now partially planted and seeds are germinating in the boiler room. Everybody seems delighted that I am glad that they are pleased. I reserve judgement because, while Solomon said that a feast of herbs where all are buddies is better than a brawl at a banquet, I cannot but feel that all herbal additions to good provender are – to employ a hendiadys – stuff-and-nonsense.

C. C. L. Browne

CALLING A ROBIN
(1969)

Sir, The robin who is my garden helpmate and has been with me for some years has learned a new trick. Sometimes, when I found a tit-bit, I would, half absentmindedly, call out "Bobbiny, Bobbiny." When I saw where he was I would throw it towards him.

*Now, I can go out on the veranda and call "Bobbiny, Bobbiny,"
and the little bird will come from out of sight, perhaps 200 yards
away, for a nibble of his favourite (which has proved to be double
Gloucester cheese). Then he will give me a song. I have never before
known of a robin to respond to a human voice.*

ROGER MOLESWORTH

*Sir, It was encouraging to read of Colonel Molesworth's success
when calling his tame robin. It reminded me of the robin which I first
attracted with mealworms during the winter. I placed a few of these
on the bird table, standing a little closer each day while he came to
take them. I then had some on the lid of the tin, which I held myself
on the hanging bird table.*
*There was much hesitation and at last one wild dash and he had
one. Eventually I had only to whistle and he would come to me from
nowhere, so to speak, and feed on mealworms or fishing grubs as I
held them out to him. He would sometimes sing. He always
squeezed the worm at first at one end, then at the other, two or three
times before swallowing it.*

MISS MAUD BRUCE

*Sir, I was hardly surprised to read of Colonel Molesworth's robin
responding to his voice, as we have had a similar experience. Last
summer we had two broods of robins and the parents used to bring
the young to feed at our bird table for a time. Later, only one of the
pair remained, the female, we think. She used to come to us when
we went out with grated cheese, and my husband would call her if
not in sight and she would come within arms length, calling in reply.*
*We found her many times in the house, after the young had
disappeared. She would hop around in the dining room in our
presence, almost under the nose of our golden retriever. We found her
upstairs too, in the bathroom. She has nested again this year in the
garage and is now feeding four hungry young.*

M. N. SHARPLESS

FEARLESS CAPERCAILZIE
(1943)

Sir, I think the following extracts from a letter written to me by Sir John Stirling-Maxwell from Corrour in Inverness-shire and dated May 21st will interest many of your readers:

"You will be interested to her that a pair of capercailzie have established themselves in the plantation behind the boat-house. They behave in a most extraordinary way. The cock bird seems to resent anyone coming through the wood. He waits in a tree for the boy who brings the post on a push-bike and, when he approaches, drops down and perches on the carrier attached to the handle-bars and buffets the wretched boy till he falls off or wobbles into the ditch. Then he returns to his tree satisfied with the morning's work. As we drove from the station, the cock bird descended from his tree onto the bonnet of the car and then onto the road just in front. When we got free of him, he proceeded to chase us down the road, running with his wings open and tail erect at about 25 m.p.h. With the combs above his eyes very bright and his glittering blue body, he was a remarkable and formidable sight. One day he annoyed Robertson (the head-stalker) so much that he stopped the car, picked the bird up and put him on the front seat where he was a very rude passenger, making threatening noises with his beak and flapping Robertson's face with his wings. The hen bird is nearly as tame. One of the nurses walking along the road met her, patted her on the back and picked her up. She did not resent it at all.

"These birds must have come from Ardverikie where they have been established for many years. I hope they will nest and bring up a family. They do no serious damage to trees and will be a handsome addition to our limited fauna."

This is a most extraordinary story and I can find nothing like it in any book of reference. If these birds do bring up a brood, it will be most interesting to see whether the young show the parents' fearlessness of human kind. Red deer calves, if found before they have heard any warning from their mother, will follow a man home and suck his fingers. And I believe that small ducklings are quite fearless if caught in the same conditions.

F. O. LINDLEY

THE ZOO ON THE DINNER TABLE
(1942)

One of the minor horrors of a major war is the sudden boosting of food-stuffs normally relegated to the pig-pail or the compost heap. It is in no such war-time make-do spirit, however, that I, as something of a gourmet, wish to enlist for a few moments the attention of the cultured, sophisticated diner. It is rather to point out a few of the delightful dishes which wait those willing to throw off the fetters of prejudice, and realise that none but the brave deserve the fare.

Frank Buckland, once a highlight of *The Field*, seriously questioned whether any animal was definitely uneatable, though now we know for a certainty that the whole of the file-fishes (*Balistidae*) contain toxic alkalis of varying virulence. Still, a desultory reading of travel books will serve to convince that hundreds of animals that are mere curios in our country provide the daily menu in their native lands. Paris has twice been forced to eat her Zoo – and may have done so again for all we know – but those gastronomic hazards recorded by Labouchère and others were rather matters of necessity than choice.

In the course of some thirty-four years steady Zoo-trotting I have been privileged to sample a selection of exhibits that have met with violent deaths and have been accorded a clean bill of health by the Zoological Society's prosector. The "findings" can be briefly tabulated thus:

Primates of any kind, despite all recommendations, have been rigidly eschewed – purely on sentimental grounds. Of insectivora, the hedgehog is the only really palatable member –

not unlike young pork; Indian fruit bat, for all that it is only eaten by 'untouchables' suggests the choicest chicken. All the smaller rodents (bar the common rat) resemble rabbit, and, once skinned, deceive the eye and nose equally with the palate. The giants of the order, coypu, beaver and capybara, suggest a blend of beef and jugged hare, and much the same applies to the dark-fleshed fish-eaters, such as seal and porpoise.

The odour of all pure carnivores has been sufficient to preclude admission to the cuisine. All antelope – with Indian black buck at their head – may rank as venison. Zebra supersedes giraffe, and both are much like a horse. The only tasty part of elephant is the foot – a most delicious brawn; whilst kangaroo fully justifies the pre-war price of 17/6 per lb. in bottled form. Bear and badger are lordly substitutes for beef.

An animal's food, of course, determines the quality of its flesh, and, whilst a mixed, fish, or vegetarian diet provides excellent results, a carnivorous one has quite the reverse effect. The Sudanese warrior who devours lion flesh does so rather in the hope of thus acquiring the lion's courage than from a *bon vivant*'s point of view.

Few Zoo birds have graced my own table, and, of these, penguin, brush turkey and flamingo easily head the list. Emu and ostrich provide quantity rather than quality. A single ostrich thigh yields over twenty pounds of rather tough and tasteless beef. But *flamingo* – no wonder the bird needs all the protection the Empire Fauna Society can afford!

The mere suggestion of eating reptiles will, I know, produce in many a state akin to hysteria. But where would the Lord Mayor be without his turtle, or, in peace-time, some of our most exclusive hotels if they failed to import Middle West chicken terrapin for their transatlantic guests. Iguana and alligator regularly feature in the New York market, and a company lately floated in Florida does a roaring trade in tinned rattle snake. Personal experience has found all the larger lizards – iguana, monitor and tegu – similar to chicken, whilst crocodile, gently casseroled, is virtually indistinguishable from veal. Frog and axodotal would not be so extensively farmed if market demands did not well repay the outlet.

Fish is too vast a subject to be dealt with here, but it is worth noting and deploring that even in war-time, out of the two hundred native kinds that could be eaten and enjoyed, not more than a dozen find any favour with the public. Sufficient answer perhaps to any who may doubt that we are, these days, easily the best fed folk in Europe.

With regard to insects I can speak first hand only of the locust – and the cochineal bug. Locust is far superior to shrimp. Molluscs, like fish, are too big a subject to be even glanced at here, and like fish, are hedged about with a mass of the most foolish prejudice. Why, for example, should mussels be associated with shirt sleeves, and an old cloth cap – but *moules marinières* with tails and white waistcoat, or at least the old school tie? Glancing at the above, coypu, grey squirrel, emu, rhea and Bennet's wallaby might well be bred for regular consumption in this country.

Still, all this is but humbly following in the footsteps of the great master, Frank Buckland – and the London Zoological Society itself. For one of the Society's aims was to add new and useful creatures to the nation's adopted fauna. But though it originated the once vast poultry movement, it never (as it hoped to do) made curassow rank with turkey, or the eland hold an equally honoured place with beef. It founded the Acclimatisation Society, which held some daring dinners at various London hotels, and a special horse flesh banquet (at the Langham Hotel in 1868), but of this even the dauntless Buckland wrote, the wealth of "gee gee dishes," however skilfully presented, one and all diffused "the aroma of a horse in a perspiration."

But Buckland's private enterprises knew no bounds. Inured as a child to all kinds of weird foods at his famous father's board – in Christchurch deanery – he embarked on fried fieldmouse and many other unusual side entrées when a schoolboy at Rugby. In 1863 he became a sort of honorary vet to the Zoo, and fairly let himself go. Considering that he was a medical man, he sampled all and sundry with a frightening indifference to the cause of death, and once insisted on tasting some "chops" from a panther that had been fourteen days interred. During his seventeen years' residence at 37, Albany Street, he must have sampled everything that died in the adjacent Zoo, to say nothing of what he discovered scouring the coasts and seaports as first Commissioner of Fisheries. He died eventually from overwork, not as a martyr to experiment. Almost his last act was to bribe the local dustman (himself being then under medical supervision) to sample a gigantic deep-sea oyster. The dustman, we are told, tried one bite, then fled, leaving the remains of the *bonne bouche* together with the bribe.

No. 37, Albany Street has happily survived the blitz, and, thanks to representations made by the Zoo Council, will in the near future be garnished by the LCC with a brass plate commemorating the man who made New Zealand the angler's paradise, and set our home fisheries on their present basis. The great Buckland could be with us now to point the way to many a tasty meat dish, gathered without trouble – and without coupons.

L. R. BRIGHTWELL

SEXING BY WEIGHT
(1942)

Sir, Referring to Mr. J. A. Miles's interesting article in The Field *on "Sexing Day-old Chicks," I wonder if any of your readers have tried the following experiment.*

If you swing a weight, pendulum fashion, over an animal the same sex as yourself, the weight will continue to swing straight to and fro, but if the sexes are opposite, the pendulum will after a few minutes assume a circular motion.

I have tried this dozens of times with domestic animals and have successfully determined the sexes of young geese by its means. Any bit of string a couple of feet long and any small weight will answer the purpose, but in swinging the weight, care should be taken to hold the hand perfectly steady.

CHARLES C. DALLAS

[Strange as this may sound, it is so. Is there perhaps some connection between this and "dowsing"? – Ed]

THE DUNMOW FLITCH
(1860)

Sir, Will you, through the medium of your valuable paper, give me some information on "The Dunmow Flitch." – Monaghan

"Monaghan" will find a long and rather amusing account of this old custom in a book entitled "Hone's Every-day Book." I believe it is necessary that the happy couple who claim the flitch should be able to declare on oath that they have been married a year and a day without once differing in opinion on any subject. And I once was told of a husband and wife who, asserting their right to the prize, had then and there a dispute as to the best mode of cooking the first piece: the lady vowing she would have it boiled for dinner, and her lord and master strongly asserting his determination to have some broiled for his breakfast, thus leading the judge to suspect that conjugal differences of opinion between them were not quite so rare as they would have wished to make it appear, and that the "flitch," that year, at least, had been unworthily bestowed. Query, Has it ever been truthfully claimed?

FIREFLY

SLACK LINES
(1938)

I sometimes believe in the malice of fate
And that I am its butt and buffoon,
When I lose all my brown trout by striking too late
And my salmon by striking too soon.

There can be no other good reason, I think,
For the face which I frequently note,
That my fly always floats when I want it to sink,
And sinks when I want it to float.

The water is always too clear or too brown,
And the wind always sells me a pup
By blowing upstream when I want to fish down
And down when I want to fish up.

And when I'm alternately watching my flies
And watching my foothold all day,
The fish look away when I want them to rise,
And rise when I'm looking away.

But all my reverses their antidote breed
In the hope which will never grow stale,
That if often I fail when my betters succeed,
I may some day succeed when they fail.

COLIN ELLIS

June

LINING THE TENNIS COURT
(1876)

Lawn tennis being so popular a game, and various means for marking out the courts having been suggested, I have lately tried marking the service and base lines with white feathers over the whitening lines, wing feathers of white swans, geese or ducks, split down the middle, and tightly pinned down with hairpins, lengthways.

This plan is far preferable to whitening alone, which washes out with rain. The straight lines are generally visible, but the base and service lines are not so easily seen from the opposite court when marked with whitening.

The feathers always look white, and are not damaged by weather. I never found them to interfere with the balls bouncing, or the worse for walking over. The whole court could be marked in this way.

My ground, being an old bowling green, is very level and shows the feathers to great advantage. My feathers have been down a month and are as good as ever.

W. C. S.

REAL LAWN TENNIS
(1969)

We have tackled our hoofprint-studded tennis lawn lately. The first step was to lift every bruised turf, pack it up and replace the divot, and this has given us three months' intermittent work. Next came the arranging for the area to be permanently enclosed by horse-proof, chain-link netting, and that has still to be done.

Then we trotted a machine around which leaks a smelly mixture supposed to encourage grass while suppressing daisies, as a preliminary to passaging a powered roller over those roughnesses which prevent the lawn from being a true, plane surface except in so far as it conforms to the earth's curvature.

It took some while to find a place which would lease me such a roller, for the first three all said that they no longer stocked them as they were too delicate. But the fourth plant-hire firm produced one, gave me instruction and said that if its quarter ton weight was insufficient I could, by pulling a lever, cut in the thumper which would raise the pressure to several tons.

They were not sure what the thumper was but fancied that the manufacturers had caged in a tiny but very heavy man who, if adequately stimulated, would jump up and down vehemently. After which, they drove it up the ramp and into my horse-trailer, sniggering the while.

How anyone could describe the apparatus as delicate passes comprehension. Its superstructure is hewn out of a solid block of iron, and driving it is like long-reining a Churchill tank. Controlling it on the flat would give anyone biceps like Mr. World.

The cross-country journey to get it to the court left a trail akin to the path of a tornado, for twice it took charge and went waddling off course over a manure-heap and through a wilderness of shrubs. But I wrestled it on to the lawn and all went well until I was foolhardy enough to cut in the thumper.

I had never visualized so vast a vibration, for it pervaded everything. I was struck by palsy, the landscape danced in front of my quivering eyeballs and the machine advanced in standing leaps, each of which left a concave impression on the lawn. The court would have become corrugated if the tremors had not bounced the carburettor float off its seating and choked the engine dead, and after that I struck all thumpers off my calling-list.

The lawn now has a level depressed look about it and time will show whether all the grass has been killed by the juggernaut. It is a pity that my kicking serve off the tree-root in the south-east corner will lose in effectiveness, but our work will result in a game where it will no longer be madness to let the ball bounce.

On the whole, the mighty machine has done us well. But anyone tempted to experiment with one would be wise to take a physical fitness course first or at least satisfy himself that he can do 50 consecutive press-ups, for his delicacy of constitution should not exceed that of the machine.

C. C. L. Browne

EPSOM
(1853)

Few would think that this little village, ordinarily the quietest of the quiet, had once rivalled Bath and Tonbridge [*sic*] in the number, fashion, and splendour of its visitors. But so it was in 1650, when thousands resorted to Epsom Wells to try the mineral water cure of good Mr. Parkhurst.

The mineral spring is about half-a-mile west of the village and was the first of the kind discovered in England. It was accidentally found in the reign of Elizabeth, in consequence of cattle refusing to drink the water. The fame of the Epsom spring soon spread into Europe, and from it was prepared salts, the demand for which was greater than the supply. The concourse of families and foreigners resorting to the well was so great that Mr. Parkhurst, then lord of the manor, enlarged the first building by erecting a ballroom; the village increased rapidly, and yet could not contain all the visitors.

About the beginning of the last century, however, the waters gradually lost their reputation through the knavery of an apothecary of the name of Livingstone, who built a house, with an assembly-room, and then by means of balls, concerts, and other amusements, contrived to draw the company from the old well; and at length, getting the lease of the place, shut it up. The new water, however, was found not to possess the virtues of the old, and Epsom began to be deserted, until Mr. Parkhurst, at the expiration of Livingstone's lease, repaired the buildings of the old well and had public breakfasts, with horse-racing every Monday in the summer. But Fashion proved as inconstant to Epsom as she has to a hundred other favourites, and in 1804 the Well-house was pulled down, and a dwelling erected on its site.

The earliest mention of Epsom races is made by Clarendon in 1648, when "a meeting of the Royalists was held under the pretence of a horse race." Since 1730, the meetings have been continued annually; but until the establishment of "The Oaks" in 1779, the prizes were of the humblest description, small plates which were contested in the running of heats.

The Derby and the Oaks are generally known to derive their titles from the grandfather of the present Lord Derby, and his beautiful seat in the county of Surrey. His lordship took the greatest interest in the Turf; and it is somewhat singular that the first Oaks was won by Bridget, the property of that nobleman. The race originated when Lady Elizabeth Hamilton, subsequently Countess of Derby, gave a positive refusal in the first instance to his lordship's proposals of marriage, thinking that his Grace the Duke of Dorset was in the act of falling captive to her charms. This hope, however, was doomed to be disappointed, and upon the renewal of the attentions of the scion of the house of Stanley, she accepted the offer.

Determined that her nuptials should be signalised by a scene of unusual splendour, a *fête champêtre* was contrived, upon which several thousands were expended. Among other attractions, a musical drama, written by General Burgoyne of Saratoga celebrity, entitled "The Maid of the Oaks" was produced, and at this fête it was resolved that the Oaks should be established to perpetuate the festivities. This occurred in 1777, although the race, in accordance with the design, could not be brought off for two years afterwards.

In 1780, the first Derby, with 36 subscribers, was run for, and won by Sir C. Bunbury's Diomede, with a field of just nine. The smallest number that were ever saddled for "The Blue Riband of the Turf" was in 1794, when four only appeared at the post, and Lord Grosvenor's Dædalus proved the winner. The largest field was in 1851, when 33 jumped off as the flag dropped, and Teddington bore away the prize.

The Grand Stand was built in 1829 at a cost of £20,000, affording ample space for 5000 spectators. On a bright clear day, the views from the roof are extensive, Windsor Castle, Claremont, St. Paul's Cathedral, and the towers of Westminster Abbey being distinctly visible.

This week, all the world and his wife will be there, the race-day par excellence of the world; for in no other country but England, and on no other day in the three hundred and sixty-five can such a spectacle be seen as Epsom Downs will then present.

ANON.

A FOX AND FLEAS
(1969)

Sir, My elder brother was riding round our grazing bullocks when he noticed an old dog fox, about which our village had been comp-laining, performing amazing antics in an adjoining field.

Hiding himself behind a high piece of hedge he watched this fox methodically collecting thistle-down and sheep's wool from the barbed wire fence surrounding the field. When he had collected enough he held the ball, the size of a small tennis ball, between his front teeth and trotted off to a pond in the corner of the meadow, jumped in and swam round and round, holding his muzzle clear of the water, then jumped out and dropped his ball on the grass and away.

On examination, the ball was full of fleas. Is this a common practice or only to be seen in the Shires around midsummer?

R. C. L. MOULD

(1940)

Sir, There has often been correspondence in this and other journals for and against the statement that the fox, when pestered by fleas, will back into water holding a piece of sheep's wool in his mouth, and finally release the wool with the fleas which have run into it.

Sheikh Zafir, of the School of Oriental and African Studies, has just shown me an article in an Arabic anthology which bears on the problem, and I am indebted to him for helping in its translation. The article was written by Ibshaihy, who died in AD 1446.

"The fox is clever and has many tricks and stratagems when seeking his livelihood. He performs one of his amusing tricks when he is overpowered by fleas. He goes down to water, plucks out a little of his fur, and gathering it into his mouth enters the water. The fleas fly slowly until they collect in the tuft of fur and he throws it away in the water and goes out.

"He sometimes pretends to die, inflating his stomach and raising his paws in the air, so that he seems to be indeed dead, until some animal approaches him, when he springs upon it and catches it."

O. H. MYERS

(1933)

Sir, There have recently been some doubts raised in the minds of the readers of a great evening paper concerning a fox ridding itself of vermin. I have communicated, therefore, with the naturalist who was fortunate enough to see the occurrence, which took place on the River Windrush, near Burford.

From the opposite bank he saw the fox gather wool from a wire fence on which sheep had rubbed, then submerge himself.

Some townsmen are apt to put a very small limit on the intelligence of wild animals, I think because they do not have the opportunity which is afforded to countrymen to study wild life.

Elephants, rhino and crocodiles allow birds to rid them of pests, the latter from their teeth; a badger cleans its earth with the utmost regularity. Why should the fox be laughed at for using an intelligent opportunity for cleaning itself?

For the guidance of those who are liable to underrate the intelligence of God's creatures that are less than man, may I suggest they read The Life of the Bee, *and also* The Life of the Ant, *by Maurice Maeterlinck.*

G. T. H.

CROSSING WILD CATS WITH TAME
(1934)

Although it is known that the amiable domestic cat is not of European origin, I have heard it argued that specimens with striped tabby coats must have an admixture of the blood of *Felix silvestris*. My experience leads me to doubt it.

Satan, a wild cat of purest Highland blood, came to me in June, 1930, as a young kitten, and the promptitude with which he was named and the fact that that name has never been changed, shows how his disposition was at once apparent and has remained unaltered.

Formerly widely distributed throughout the British Isles, it is not surprising that so savage a creature was brought nigh to extermination. Its extremely predatory habits led to every man's hand being against it. The war, however, ensured an amnesty for vermin throughout the length and breadth of the country, and with the younger keepers elsewhere and the elder ones otherwise employed the wild cat began to recover in numbers; certain far-seeing landowners, valuing the preservation of an interesting wild animal more than a few extra brace of grouse, gave it protection with the result that the wild cat now occurs in fair numbers in central Inverness-shire, south into Perthshire, and north into Ross-shire.

I believe my Satan is as nearly tame as any member of his untamable breed has ever been. He knows the various members of my family and is not afraid of us, coming to the side of his cage to take food, but the presence of a stranger will make him retreat, hissing and spitting, into his sleeping-box. When hungry he watches for me quite keenly, and will accept meat from my hand, but one has to beware of a blow from his well-armed paw – he can scratch, as I know to my cost! So far, so good, but he has been untouchable since his kitten days, and the least unexpected happening will transform him into a spitting, raving lunatic.

When he arrived as a tiny helpless mite I got a female domestic kitten to bring up with him, and he became much attached to Beauty, as she was named. He has never wavered in this devotion, nor taken the slightest interest in any other female. When I introduced a strange lady into the cage he attacked her furiously. His conduct supports the idea that the wild cat is monogamous in its habits. Beauty has had four litters of kittens of which Satan has been the sire; and despite the fact that she is a long-haired cat of semi-Persian type, her markings being the blotched type of tabby, every kitten has been just like its sire: all have been short-coated, striped tabbies, with the heavily ringed tail of the true wild cat.

The first family were brought up in the house and treated as much-pampered pets, yet they early developed many peculiarities, being a queer mixture of affectionateness and shyness. They also betrayed a great desire to get aloft, and were climbing almost before they could toddle. Although fed in the house, and in every way encouraged to stay indoors, they generally slept in the jasmine upon the walls, and were often to be seen playing on the housetop. They began to take too great an interest in the poultry, and before they were half-grown had got into serious mischief, having finally to be shut up in a pheasant aviary – minus pheasants! – to keep them from doing further damage. Yet their mother is a most blameless and charming cat, with hardly an idea beyond a little mouse-hunting. The hybrids were ready to hunt anything and everything, and knew not where to draw the line.

A tom cat from a succeeding litter was an even more interesting character. Like his sire in all details of appearance, the Imp of Satan had engaging manners, but was even more desperately sporting than his elder sisters. He would follow me for miles across country, hunt and catch rabbits like a dog, but there came an evening when he slipped away from me, spent a night out, got into a poultry run and killed four fowls. Since then all trips have been abandoned, and the poor Imp of Satan spends his days behind wire netting, in company with his equally unreliable sisters.

It is thought of the behaviour of these cats which makes me doubt the theory that fireside pussies with striped coats owe the pattern of their jackets to *silvestris* blood. Wild cat blood means other things besides a striped coat; it means a desire to be up and off, hunting anything and everything that can be met with, from field mice to geese! No, if there was ever any admixture of wild cat blood in the veins of our harmless little puss it has long been bred out.

FRANCES PITT

KISS OF LIFE FOR A CAT ...
(1972)

Sir, A few days ago my man Tom saved his cat's life with the kiss of life. The cat was in the habit of sitting on the cover of an indoor tank of tropical fish, the water being heated by electricity. Probably having seen the electric lead to the tank move, and thinking it was something to play with, the cat bit it.

There was a flash and the cat, with his jaws clamped to the lead, went stiff as a board, and appeared to be dead. Tom disconnected the lead, grabbed the cat to his chest, massaged it and blew down its throat. The cat recovered.

That he knew what to do was not surprising as he himself had been electrocuted two weeks earlier and was saved by the kiss of life. That he had the presence of mind to put the correct drill into effect appears highly commendable.

I wonder how many people know that the kiss of life for drowning or electrocution has to be administered immediately (within four minutes) to be of avail.

R.S. KING

... SAVING THE LIFE OF A MASTER
(1902)

Sir, In the middle of Eling Vicarage, Hampshire, there is a life-size figure of a Newfoundland dog resting on an oval plinth, the monument altogether being about 6 ft. high. From the dates it appears that the dog was in the possession of his new master, whose life he had saved, for twenty-one years, and must have been something more than a puppy at the beginning of that time. The inscription is as follows:

In memory
of a Newfoundland dog
Formerly called Tiger, afterwards Friend,
Eminently qualified

By acuteness of scent, quickness of eye,
Strength of body, and peculiar sagacity,
For every duty of his species,
Who on the fourteenth day of October 1789,
When one to whom he was yet a stranger,
But was in a short time to be his master,
Had unconsciously been carried out of his depth
While bathing in the sea at Portsmouth,
and being unable to swim
His strength became exhausted and his senses overpowered
By long struggling with the waves,
Rushed spontaneously to his assistance
Seized him by the hair,
Brought him cautiously and steadily to the shore
And thus rescued him from imminent death,
From gratitude
... preserver of ...
... guardian of ...
... Phillips
Caused this monument to be erected
Over his remains which are here deposited
AD 1810

T. THISTLE

ROTTEN ROW
(1860)

O, wad some power the giftie gie us,
To see oursels as others see us. – BURNS

I am confident that exhibited daily in the ride in Hyde-park there are more extraordinary specimens of the bad, or, perhaps, I should rather say the ludicrous school of equestrianism to be seen there than ever entered the inventive brains of a Ducrow, a Batty or a Cooke, whose "Scenes in the Circle" are quite eclipsed by the al fresco performers to be seen free, gratis, for nothing, any fine afternoon in Rotten-row.

The ladies, of course, take the precedence, and I must do them the justice to say that they are less open to the accusation of making themselves conspicuous by the assumption of peculiarities in dress and manner than the gentlemen, though they certainly show a weakness in favour of gay colours and feathers. I can venture to draw the attention to no less than five different varieties of performers, and each fair lady can examine herself as to which of these classes she belongs.

1. *The shape of jelly*. Many fair equestrians seem to think that the more motion they can give their bodies while on horseback the more graceful and attractive is their appearance. That, I can assure them, is a very great mistake, and the idea that a lady's head is, as it were, only tacked on loosely to her shoulders, and in some danger of coming off, is anything but agreeable to the spectator or becoming to the fair lady. I am, however, far from advocating an unnatural stiffness.

2. *The spread eagle* appears with her elbows held out alarmingly far from her side, and her hands well out before her, so that her body is as much disunited as it well can be. This style seems adopted for the purpose of display, and, while challenging criticism, seems to express the words, "This is the way to do it"; and as it is so stiff, and far too elaborate, it is not by any means to be commended.

3. *The corkscrew* is a much inferior variety to the last, and the specimens, I am sorry to say, are rather more numerous. If ladies will not endeavour to sit straight on their horses, so as to be able to look straight before their horse's head, and while sitting crooked try to rise to the trot, the corkscrew movement is inevitable; and no perfection of figure, taste in dress, or beauty in the animal on which she is mounted, can by any possibility render a corkscrew otherwise than exceedingly ungraceful.

4. *The look-at-me* seat is that practised by a few young ladies who, when not going at a smart – extra smart – canter, keep their horses in a perpetual fret; and the foam-covered bit and restless movements of the animal make the spectator sometimes think that the fair equestrian "provokes the caper that she seems to chide." I am aware that this appearance is

sometimes caused by natural fretfulness of temper, and at other times by the saddle having shifted in the course of the afternoon's ride so as to become uneasy to the horse; but from the smile of conscious enjoyment that often bedecks the face of his fair burden, I am inclined to think that the horse gets frequent sly hints that these capricious movements are not disagreeable to her.

5. *The quite at home seat* requires no remarks from me, except to congratulate the fair on the possession of that which is in itself so graceful and becoming, for a lady with a good figure, well dressed, properly mounted, and with a good seat on horseback, seldom appears to more advantage; and long may they continue to practise and enjoy that graceful exercise which gives brilliancy to the eyes and complexions, and healthful vigour to the frames of England's fairest daughters.

I could enlarge upon many other varieties of the equestrian order to be seen every day in Rotten-row, such as the "would-be military" and "the tongs"; readers will perceive that in Rotten-row they will find an inexhaustible amount of humorous scenes out of the circle to amuse them and a spectacle which, all in all, cannot be equalled anywhere.

CHASSEUR

GREY SQUIRRELS
(1930)

Sir, I have read with interest many of the letters published by you re grey squirrels, and I can fully endorse what has been said about the way in which the red squirrels have disappeared.

This house is surrounded by a wood of about 50 acres, and there used to be plenty of red squirrels until the grey ones appeared several years ago. Now we have not a red squirrel left, and anyone who wishes to preserve the red squirrels should immediately wage war on any grey squirrels which appear in their woods.

During the last year 220 grey squirrels have been killed in this wood – 48 of these were shot in one day – and I think it might interest your readers to know the steps which were taken on that occasion. Two men were armed with shot guns, and two others carried a ladder and a long pole with which all the nests within reach were poked own, and the squirrels which came out of the nests were shot by the men standing on either side of the tree. Other nests out of reach were shot through. The result is that during the last fortnight only two squirrels have been seen.

GEORGE L. WOOD

Sir, The grey squirrel does not cross with our English red squirrel. The grey is a much stronger animal, and its method of attacking the red is by biting out the testicles – consequently the red females do not breed and die without issue.

G. PERCY ASHMORE

Sir, Mr. John W. Young says that in the Eastern, Southern and Middle States of America, the grey squirrel is esteemed as a delicacy, and that it is generally roasted when used for food. If the grey squirrel in England is really good to eat and this fact were broadcast, I think its fate would be sealed.

We have shot nine in my garden within the last two months, and a neighbouring farmer has shot about 30. He was led to do this by seeing a grey squirrel sitting in a corn field nibbling the stalks till the ears fell within reach.

If any of your readers could give further information about the value of the grey squirrel as a food in this country and methods of cooking, I would certainly publish the information locally, as the grey squirrel is becoming a real pest around here.

K. HELY HUTCHINSON

Sir, If your correspondent Mr Hutchinson will cut up the grey squirrel as follows, shoulders, legs and back, and dip them in egg and bread crumb (as he would his filleted fish) and fry in butter, he will have one of the daintiest little dishes he has ever eaten. Or, if he can get enough at one time to make into a pie, as he would young rabbits, he will not trouble about rabbit pie again.

I have killed hundreds in Canada, and cooked them myself in this way. We never see one in Herefordshire, so if Mr. Hutchinson can spare a couple out of his next bag, could he send them to me.

THOMAS VALE

"BRONZED"
(1935)

The beauty specialists of Mayfair, always working well ahead of time, are busy with a new bronze nail varnish that women are to use instead of brilliant red for shooting parties in Scotland this year. The colour of autumn leaves, it is guaranteed not to disturb the grouse or the eyes of the stern host.

ANON.

WATER MUSIC
(1969)

Ripples on the pond's face
Have cracked the quiet sky,
And troubled the calm willow boughs.
I have seen them lie
Unmoving all a summer hour,
Close to the water's lip,
Every leaf a silver ghost
Brushing its own green tip,
And when a bird, alighting, sings,
Drops of sound let fall
Join the gleaming water
Nor break its peace at all.
Only in dim tree-depths there
Note for sweet note,
Quivers, ripples,
A shadowy-feathered throat.

MARY JULIAN

July

WATCHING FLOWERS OPEN
(1971)

Sir, At this season I like to take visitors into my garden in the evenings to watch the evening primroses opening.

At 8.30 pm the buds due to open that evening are tightly folded, like well-packed parachutes. At about 8.45 pm the first glimpses of yellow petals are seen, as the bud swells.

Then, suddenly, the bud bursts, sometimes with a slight pop which persons with keen hearing claim to be able to hear. The sepals zip back, and the delicate, lemon-coloured petals expand visibly.

Some of my evening primroses are 6 ft. high, with numerous flower spikes. On each spike about two blooms open each evening.

They last one day only, but the succession goes on until at least the end of August.

RALPH WHITLOCK

HIVING THE BEES
(1971)

What follows should not be read by apiarists. I admire them in the same remote manner that I respect holders of the George Cross, but, under pressure, I cannot but admit that I think they are the Afflicted of Allah and hence untouchable and probably unstingable. I write to warn normal fathers composed of sensitive flesh and blood to have no truck with casual swarms of bees. As in certain situations at golf, sweep aside or press down but do not pick up.

Our latest swarm was nobody's fancy, so we shook them into a box, inverted it, stood it on the ground with one side slightly jacked up and fled. Two days later we had acquired a vast hive, cleared a space for it under the limes and had to manoeuvre 10,000 trigger-happy insects into their new home.

First came the expert wearing a space-suit, followed by my wife in a rather more heterodox form of body armour except for nylon-clad ankles. My daughters had ski-ing jackets and muslin toques and I was the back-stop in an old steel helmet which supported a shrimping-net whose shaft hung down my spine. The way was clear for a hideous tragedy and I wished I had thought to bring binoculars so that I could give a clear account of it later to the coroner.

I could not quite see, but I think the inhabitants of the box were first mildly kippered before being toted to their new home in which was hung as bait a frame with honey. The box was dumped in the top, wedged round with newspaper to make escape improbable, and the bees were told to like it or lump it. Strangely, they chose the first course.

Two days later, I came on my youngest daughter sitting by the landing-board rapping on it to bring out the sentries and then offering them a honey-covered hand. Daughters must be braver than fathers.

C. C. L. BROWNE

TEACHERS AND PREACHERS WITH A FLY-ROD
(1970)

In his *Book of the Dry Fly*, G. A. B. Dewar wrote: "For my part, I am inclined to believe that the best way to become an accomplished dry fly fisherman is to steer clear of teachers and preachers, either in the book, or in the flesh, get down to the water, look out for rising trout, and hammer away until one is at length hooked and landed" – which brought a waspish response from Fred Shaw, then pioneering his fly-casting school in London.

Sometimes I think Dewar was right, yet when I visit the Game Fair and watch that almost miraculous casting of international or world champions, I think he was wrong. Then I remember Skues, lord of the Ichen and one of the greatest fly-fishermen who ever dispatched a fly upon the waters. When tempted to take lessons he always said to himself, "No, no, my son. Let well alone. You may catch a trout now and then with your amateur, anyhow, hugger-mugger style. If you took lessons and acquired perfection you might catch none."

Teachers in the book, all worthy men and full of good intentions, can pave the way, if not to hell, then to a fair imitation of purgatory; though if this be the region in which the taught reside, it is usually because they have learnt too grimly, misapplying the teacher's principles. For one such despairing soul, enmeshed in the coils of his casting, salvation lay in a few moments of watching a good caster, without realizing that he was being deliberately taught. This beginner had fallen into an unholy mess, flinging his line back with such gusto that it was impossible to check his rod. The line dropped into the bushes behind him or flopped, exhausted from its punishment, in tangles on the water at his feet.

A nearby angler who could no longer bear the performance or the profanity wandered up and said: "That's a nice looking rod. How does it feel?" At which the demented learner, after disentangling himself, reeled in and offered the rod, replying a little sheepishly: "Not too bad, but a bit stiff for me."

The experienced angler made three or four beautiful casts, the line rolling out sweetly and straight, the fly kissing the water. The tyro observed secretly but well. This man did not hurl the line behind him with such force that the rod went over with it, but flicked it back with no fuss, barely using his forearm. The rod came alive; the forward cast, made at that exact moment when the line tugged on the rod, was a light, controlled sweep, followed through until the forearm was nearly parallel with the water.

Revelation came in those few moments. The novice learnt, as perhaps he would never have learnt from books, the difference between casting and thrashing. The errors in style, the needless energy, were made plain. Within hours his casting became respectable; within weeks it was good. Now, two seasons later, it is excellent. And he never realized he had been the subject of a successful confidence trick.

The angler handed back the rod, smiled as sweetly as he had cast, remarked on the rod's virtues and, being a man of tact, made himself scarce. Dewar's advice would have brought this beginner little joy. Perhaps the mistakes would eventually have been overcome, but not without the expense of much time and at the cost of many pounds per square inch of rising blood pressure. Perhaps they would not have been completely overcome, for it is a precept of casting teachers that early mistakes tend to stick.

Skues's "anyhow, hugger-mugger style" was as near perfect as any self-taught man could hope to achieve. He was a law unto himself, but his remarks on acquiring perfection had a strong general relevance, if by perfection we mean an unfailing ability to lay on the water a dead straight line and cast.

I know a fisherman who is a joy to behold; his actions are so co-ordinated as to seem almost robot-like, and if that suggests something inhuman it is a wrong description, for there is nothing inhuman about him, and everything of graceful movement about his casting. But he is too good: he cannot cast a crooked line. On calm water he is a wizard; where there is drag he remains a novice.

I suspect that Skues had such a peril in mind, though he need not have worried, for he knew every trick. For my part, if I may adapt Dewar, I am inclined to believe that the best way to become an accomplished caster is to steer towards a good teacher. The best one I ever knew was a poacher. He never preached. He could not, since his verbal instructions were confined to a few unprintable phrases.

TORRENTIS

THE ITINERANT DOG BREAKER
(1920)

He was on his way to the races, I think, and entered the motor omnibus with his wife, a dog, and a sack, about half-way along the road. Man, woman, and dog were a varminty looking trio, all game to the backbone. The woman had the most complete cast in her eyes that I have ever seen. The pupil in each eye seemed to be quite down in the right-hand corner. She looked at you, so to say, round both corners. The man had the brightest possible eyes; otherwise he was inconspicuous. Both were spare, middle-aged, shabbily but not ill-clad. A remark about the dog opened the man's lips, and he talked without ceasing for twenty miles. "Yes," he said, "that 'ull be the best lurcher in these parts, when his time comes, that's to say, for he's only a young 'un."

"And how old will he be?" "Six months, in a few days, and he'll pull down two hares out of three. He'll be a rare one for the rabbit coursing. That's to say, in Wales and these parts. He'd be no good up Yorkshire and Lancashire way." And then he explained that the dog was half greyhound, half Welsh collie – that in Wales it was a matter of weights, but up the country a dog must be pure bred. He went on to speak of rabbit coursing. Why should the rich man course his hares, but then try to prevent the poor man from coursing rabbits?

The dog was a long, lathy, black and white lurcher, like a greyhound cut down, but with rounder loins, a far more intelligent face, and delightful eyes. "Breeder?" Yes, he had bred most everything, chiefly dogs, fighting-cocks, and pigeons. He used to breed the English terrier, but they "ran out" as he expressed it. They spoilt the breed by mating it with the fox-terrier. "Lor," he said. "I had a bit of fun out of that. There was Sir Harry's man. He used to take the dogs a walk round the hill every morning at a quarter to seven, and I had the best of the fox-terriers for my bitch. I had five pounds each for the poops," which word he pronounced like a Yorkshireman, but I think he was mid-country born and bred.

Then he talked of training dogs, especially collies. The old English sheep-dog was too slow, but he seemed to be especially fond of the Welsh collie; knew them best, perhaps. The best way to train the pups was this: "You chain them to the bitch. Your word is law to her. You just start 'em on the hill-side, after the sheep, and her'll larn them. She've got to do what you've a mind to, and they've got to do what her've a mind to."

The talk turned on bulldogs and dog fights. "They trained 'em for it, made 'em go for the tenderest mark, choked 'em off every other. There was a fight up at — public house in the early morning – tug, tug, tug – twenty-five minutes – terrible cruel, that was, terrible cruel. But the detectives came down on them, and Billy he got nine months, and Jim and Jerry six months apiece. Ah, it was cruel, terrible cruel." As to cock fighting, "You couldn't beat a cross between a game fowl and a pheasant. What could be braver than a pheasant?" I've heard this before, in another part of the country, about the best fighting bird being a cross between a game fowl and a pheasant, but am inclined to doubt it. "As to cock fighting, the Hon.—, son of Lord —, told me some years ago that it was as common as ever. He wanted me to board out some of his gamecocks, stags we call them in our part of the world. I said I was afraid they'd eat my hens. Anyhow, we still breed plenty of game fowls, and our people don't breed what they can't sell of it afterwards. Many a laugh we had over that."

And so we came to our journey's end, and said goodbye, much to my regret, and the grim, lean, downlooking wife, and the little, rat-faced, bright-eyed man, with their bundle, and their bright, intelligent, half-bred dog, walked off, and I saw them no more. Good sports, they looked, all three of them alert, open-air creatures, man, woman, and dog.

C. S. J.

FIRST MESMERISE YOUR RABBIT
(1970)

As a child, I was once told by an old lady well versed in country lore that if I saw a rabbit disturbed by a stoat and walked round it slowly in decreasing circles I should eventually get near enough to stroke it or even pick it up. Fear would paralyse it so completely that it could not run away.

I had no chance to test this theory until, years later, I was attending a course at Flatford Mill, in Suffolk. It was a warm summer evening and we were walking home from the river across the fields to the mill. Suddenly we heard the high-pitched scream of a rabbit attacked by a stoat. Every rabbit in sight made for its burrow, silently flashing a signal with its white tail.

It was before the days of myxomatosis and there had been dozens about a second before. Now there was none, except in the next field. Here, the rabbits along one side did not disappear. They ran a few feet, then crouched. As we approached, the same thing happened again. Though obviously disturbed by our presence, they did not go below. This used to be a familiar sign that weasels or stoats were working their burrows.

We decided to put the old lady's theory to the test. A fellow student tried first. She chose a rabbit and went towards it, cutting it off from the others; she then described a circle round it, then another and another, until at last the radius was so small that she was within touching distance. Still the rabbit did not move.

Reaching out, hardly believing it possible, she stroked its ears. Then, slipping a hand underneath it, she lifted it gently into her arms. The rest of us, standing in a group watching, thought it was dead. It remained rigid, still in the crouching position but it did not move. So, not wishing to leave it in this condition for the stoat, we decided to carry it to the mill, where we could protect it until it had recovered. As we crossed two large fields to the mill, the rabbit remained rigid in the girl's arms with no sign of movement.

Then, at the gate, its eyes lost their concentrated stare, its ears twitched suddenly, and in a flash it leapt out of her arms and disappeared into the hedge, leaving us wondering whether a rabbit's "freezing" in the face of an enemy is an instinctive act of camouflage or an attack of cramp brought on by stark terror.

Ethel Garland

FOLLOWING BUFFALO BILL
(1970)

The Royal is going Western. From Texas, Arizona and California, Sioux and Navajo Indians will thunder across the Stoneleigh ranges, and Texan cowboys will display trick riding, wagon racing and the fastest quarter horses in the world. Nothing like it has been seen in this country since Buffalo Bill brought his Wild West Show to Europe in 1887.

But whether the Stoneleigh Rodeo will live up to the spectacle by Colonel Cody remains to be seen.

His show was executed at reckless speed. It included prairie fires, stampedes, the massacre of Custer's troops, a cowboy band mounted on buffaloes, a stage-coach pursued by Indians, and the grand finale, a mountain tornado – there were wild horses and Indians in plenty, with a bonus of buffalo, deer, elk and antelope. Cowboys snatched objects from the ground at full gallop, lassoed steers and buffalo, and rode broncos that combined spines like whale bone with the explosive elements of a high-pressure pile-driver.

To qualify as a fully fledged bronco buster one had to learn "all the mysteries of rear and tear, stop and drop, lay and roll, kick and bite, on and off, under and over, heads and tails, handsprings, triple somersaults, standing on your head, diving, flip-flaps, getting left (horse leaving you 15 miles from camp with Indians in the neighbourhood) and all the funny business included in the familiar term of "bucking," according to one of Buffalo Bill's handouts.

The would-be cowboy, once he had mastered the art of gripping his horse with knees and legs, sitting low and accommodating himself to every move of the animal, would then have to learn to handle a rope, catch a calf, throw a beef steer, play with a wild bull, lasso an untamed mustang, fight off an Indian and endure daily all the dangers of a toreador.

What Buffalo Bill would have made of the Royal Show is an amusing speculation. Perhaps the mini-donkeys would remind him of the mule that once jerked loose from him and trotted off, leading its fuming rider for more than 35 miles. (Bill Cody got his revenge: he pumped the animal full of lead and left its carcase for the crows.)

There was a model farm (surely a dude ranch), and a cookery demonstration. Bill Cody's cookery consisted first of shooting his birds, then rolling them unplucked in mud and covering them with red-hot embers. When done to a turn, off came the caked mud taking the feathers with it, out fell the entrails, and the meal was ready.

Colonel Cody looked after his guests and the Stoneleigh caterers would be hard put to equal the menu laid on after the Buffalo Bill Show: Soup; whiskey with water. Fish; whiskey straight. Entrée; Crackers with pepper, salt and whiskey. Roast: Chunks of beef ribs from a whole ox, timber sauce well laced with whiskey, etcetera. The menu finished with the ominous words, "Ambulances to Order."

Then the Fashion Shows – the Prince of Plainsmen would surely shine at them in the outfit he wore to scalp the young Indian chief, Yellow Hand. For this daring, and for once partially true, exploit, the Colonel wore a magnificent Mexican suit of black velvet, slashed with scarlet and trimmed with silver buttons and lace.

It is almost impossible to sort out the truth from the legend of Buffalo Bill's exploits. Unlike the popular heroes that have grown fortuitously in folk lore, Buffalo Bill was the subject of a deliberate and skilful use of publicity. One old Western ranger who, on being challenged as to the veracity of some blood curdling exploit, said thoughtfully: "Well, it's like this, I guess I've lived out here in this Western country so long and I've told so many damn lies, that the truth is I don't know when I can believe myself." He could have been speaking for Cody.

Cody was absent from the trails when the first genuine Indian depredations began, but he destroyed more Indians through his mass slaughter of buffalo than through bullets to the hearts of Redskin braves. The decimation of the vast buffalo herds that roamed the North American plains up to the middle of the last century set in train the devastation that led to the total eclipse of the Red Indian tribesmen. For they relied on the buffaloes for the food they ate, for the milk they drank, for their clothes and for their shelter. The herds had been as much as 20 miles wide and twice as long, containing some four million head of animals, but by the end of the century the total buffalo population amounted to only a few thousand, and the Red Indian himself was almost extinct.

Buffalo Bill's method of killing was systematically to sweep great herds of buffalo into a tight knot, and by pressing the leaders hard to the left, he got the drove circling. Then shooting unerringly downwards to their hearts, he picked off those that tried to break away, leaving a welter of carcases within the perimeter of a small area. This was much appreciated by the following butcher.

It is from the fictionalized versions of Colonel Cody's adventures that we know Buffalo Bill best. His magnificent figure mounted on a snow-white stallion galloped into action weekly for more than fifty years. Buffalo Bill came into the lives of ordinary human beings in a way that Sherlock Holmes, Dan Dare, Tarzan and James Bond all failed to do.

Anyone who could afford to buy a ticket could see him ride, shoot, swing his lariat, and then after the show, they could eat and drink with the hero, finger his string of scalps and listen to his yarns.

Buffalo Bill, Buffalo Bill
Never missed and never will;
Always aims and shoots to kill
And the company pays his buffalo bill.

Buffalo Bill was not only prince of the plains – he was also a prince of publicity.

GLORIA COTTESLOE

THE DECLINE AND FALL OF BRACES
(1970)

A British institution loses support, but what would Mr. Vardon have said?

A retired Admiral I once knew could be provoked beyond endurance by the sight of what passes nowadays as fashionable male attire. "Sloppy fellow. Trousers too long. A man without braces is like a ship without a rudder – out of control, weak in the stern and a menace to everyone." An overstatement perhaps, but the custom of securing the trousers we wear for sporting occasions by means of braces has sadly diminished. But there was a time when most sportsmen were bracesmen and under-50s will be forgiven their ignorance of it. They cannot know, and may not believe, that in all but the most decorous and gentle of outdoor sports, like croquet, braces were the order of the day. Take golf, for instance: the span of years which produced Vardon, Braid, Taylor, Ray, Duncan and Mitchell. With styles and methods of play even more varied then than they are today, these great players had at least one common denominator whether, like Vardon, Duncan and Mitchell, they played in knickerbockers, or, like Braid and Taylor, they wore long trousers.

American tailors of that period were able, I fancy, as ours have learned to do nowadays, to cut trousers which enable the wearer to dispense with any visible means of support and I believe that neither Hagen nor Jones were bracesmen, although both habitually wore plus-fours. Vardon, on the other hand, thought so highly of the matter that he included advice in his *The Compleat Golfer*.

"Always use braces in preference to a belt round the waist. I never play with a belt. Braces seem to hold the shoulders together just as they ought to be. When a man plays in a belt he has an unaccustomed sense of looseness and his shoulders are too much beyond control. It is a mistake to imagine you can swing better with a belt than braces."

All the good shots I knew were bracesmen. One of them, the late Macomb Chance, found that his swing was restricted by the standard type of article then in vogue. With characteristic thoroughness he set himself to design a brace which would enable him to swing his gun free from impediment through a complete quadrant. This was achieved by means of a complex system of pulleys so that the stress on arms, shoulders and trouser buttons remained constant while the gun was aimed in any direction. There is no record of the method he used to lubricate the pulleys and other moving parts, but one can be certain that this problem was solved and that his shirt did not suffer from oil stains.

Happily, many gamekeepers are as wise as their forebears and remain loyal bracesmen despite the often lax example of their employers and their guests, some of whom have long since abandoned their braces along with their cut-throat razors. Rod fishermen, however, come into a different category because no-one has, as yet, devised a means of securing body waders without either braces or shoulder straps. Some anglers prefer the traditional button-on elastic braces to the modern one-piece garment because of the ease of adjustment, comfort and feeling of security. Incidentally, fishing in body waders allows women the privilege of sharing the same experience and wearing braces too. I do not know of any other pastime which does this (unless it be parachuting) despite the modern cult of trousers amongst women.

In my earlier days the village cricketer who appeared in white trousers secured by braces was a normal sight which aroused no comment. Nowadays, a batsman or bowler so attired would not be allowed out of the pavilion. But in those times we were more tolerant about dress for sport. No less an authority than the eminent broadcaster Mr. Freddie Grisewood, a games player of distinction, has written about a cricketer in his Oxfordshire village side, one Tiny Wells. He always turned out to bowl, not only in braces but wearing a bowler hat.

Lawn tennis has never gladly tolerated the braces-clad player. Certainly, in pre-First World War days neither the Doherty brothers, Anthony Wilding nor their contemporaries of any nationality ever appeared at old Wimbledon in braces. Photographs indicate that their waists were encircled by belts or sashes. Remarkable, perhaps, but I have never heard that any tennis player of either sex was embarrassed by a *lapsus lingerie* on the Centre Court.

Yet I do recall an instance of a tennis player, a good one too, turning out in corduroy trousers secured in the traditional way, but not at Wimbledon. This was the late Mr. Rainbow, head gardener to the first Lord Birkenhead. He would be called to the court whenever a fourth player was needed.

"Coming, m'Lord," he would respond to the call, "just let me put on me tennis slippers." Rainbow would emerge from the potting-shed attired as for his normal duties but bearing an ancient racquet and wearing white shoes, equipped and competent to hold his own in the most illustrious company.

The game of bowls furnishes us with an example of a leisurely occupation in which the wearing of braces arises, not so much from what may be termed as trouser stress as perhaps from a striving for sartorial splendour. No bowlsman worth his salt would appear on the green without them, and the more flamboyant the better. The same applies in the case of his cold-weather brother, the curling man or curlsman.

The most ardent bracesman would be unwise, however, to assert that the wearing of braces is indispensable to every form of sport. Polo players, hockeys and swimmers seem to get on happily without them, which brings me to the crux of the matter – the bracemanship code. Reduced to its basic roots the essence of this code is that, whenever possible, braces should be concealed beneath an outer garment. In the days of Vardon this was a Norfolk jacket.

More recently, although the jacket has given way to the jersey or pullover, the principle of concealment remains inviolate, but with a special licence for village cricketers, wading anglers and bowlsmen. The bracemanship code has never been, like the British Constitution, precisely formulated. Nor has it yet appeared in print. Its ethics, however, are well understood by all wearers. Failure to comply is not treated lightly, and can lead to social ostracism.

There is the tendency amongst some bracesmen, who should know better, and often the host at a country house party, to stand in front of the library fire, unfasten their coat buttons, and use their thumbs to pull the elastic forward and then, in a flaunting sort of way to let it fly back against the chest with an audible twang. This gambit, normally reserved for male gatherings, is often used in conversation to emphasize a point. A fairly harmless habit, you may think. But, unhappily, it has been exploited for their own benefit by some unscrupulous gamesmen. It is exceedingly distracting when one lines up for that vital putt to save the match on the eighteenth green to observe one's opponent fingering his braces with the realisation that, as one is about to make one's stroke, he will choose that moment to flip the elastic with unnecessary force. And I have a word of caution to those who have managed so far without braces, but who may now feel that they are worth a trial after all. To them I say, buy the best that your haberdasher can offer. Do not be put off by gaudy fakes. Insist on plenty of elasticity. Before making your choice be sure to try them on, and go on trying them on until you are assured that you have a comfortable article made of robust material which will not let you or your trousers down.

A little time and care expended in this way will amply reward you. But to qualify as a complete braceman you must go a little further. Make certain, whenever you wear your new braces for some important social or sporting occasion, that the clasps on both sides are properly adjusted and pressed home. Maladjusted braces can slip off the shoulders and expose the wearer to ridicule. Just think of your shame should this happen as you step forward to embrace the bride at a reception, or rise to your feet to make a speech at a banquet. Non-sporting occasions, I grant you, but the principle still applies.

Those who remember Latin will recall the word *bracchium* which was a measure of length, the distance between the extended arms, and of special interest to fishermen. From this original meaning comes that of something which, like straps passing over the shoulder to support trousers, secures, connects, tightens or strengthens. Any device, however ancient and simple, which does all of these vital things will, I feel confident, commend itself to the modern sportsman.

Jack Chance

HAYTIME
(1970)

Heard from the silent woods
The haytime tractors blare,
Cutting a silhouette
Of summer on the air;
Limning with movement's point
On stillness a design
Of contrast that achieves
Impact with every line.
The fullness of delight;
Green hush and golden sound,
Illuminates the script
With time seen in the round;
Both aspects summer joy
Too bright or deep to fade,
The toil and clatter sun,
The peaceful quiet shade.

J. PHOENICE

August

"BEST BEFORE"
(1860)

It is often a difficult matter to know which of a lot of birds hanging in a larder ought to be cooked first. My friend Mr. Coulson has shown me how to put a date upon each bird without using pen, ink, or pencil, and it is a very simple but useful plan.

When the birds are brought in after shooting, hold up each before you with his breast facing you, then begin to count his toes from your right towards your left, after the manner the children in the nursery play the game of "Whose little pigs are these?"

Let the claws indicate the days of the week. If the bird was shot on Monday, pull the claw off the first toe you count; if on Thursday, the claw from the fourth toe, and so on.

When the birds are subsequently examined each will bear a mark, to show immediately on what day of the week he was killed.

This plan may be known to many, but I still give it for the benefit of those who never heard of it before.

F. BUCKLAND

TO GENTLEMEN GROUSE-SHOOTERS
(1855)

One word to you. I presume your dogs are spare in flesh from work, not starvation, and that you are already wearing, and occasionally wetting through, your shooting shoes or boots. Never mind their letting in wet if old and easy. New shoes or boots are all the very de'il. Don't believe your shoemaker about fitting – no, not on his oath. On no account attempt to walk on hills and heather without some holding up nails – hobnails, not too close, or square sparrow-bills left rough, but not so rough and projecting as to impede. You cannot walk on smooth soles. I saw a gentleman on Ben Lomond the other day in boots which he called his grousing boots – I should have called them dancing pumps – no nails in them, and the consequence was that he began to slide about very amusingly; and had I not been with him he would have slidden on his beam down old Ben, as the man in the moon is said to slide down the rainbow when he has any business on earth. This pirouetting does not do with a loaded double gun in your hands. Put a pair of fresh soft stockings in your pocket, and change them at lunch time; and if you feel any part of you beginning to rub or fret, put a little oil or pomatum on, which is easily carried in the pocket on a bit of wool in a twist of paper; and if your feet ever begin to feel a sensation of rubbing and chafing, cut your shoes at once – aye, to atoms – rather than get the skin off. Change them as soon as you can. And don't let me see your fat and unexercised English dogs turning out of the railway-carriages like fat sheep or ladies' poodles. You have shooting hints galore in all the books; but these are the most pressing now, for the day is at hand, and this is the last *Field* but one published before you start. And mind, order the *Field* to be sent to you every week; better pay three years' subscription in advance than neglect even one jot or tittle of this trifling advice, which it now gives you.

UMBRA

THE SWAN AS ENGLISH FOOD
(1943)

On the Thames, from the earliest times, swans have been protected. In the reign of Edward III it was ordered that no one should keep swans unless he possessed a freehold to the value of 5 marks. This practically confined the right to keep swans to the nobility and the monastic houses, but apparently the Corporation of Henley was permitted to keep "swannys," as between 1602 and 1625 the corporation books record several gifts of them to Sir James Whitelock of Fawley Court. As late as the end of the seventeenth century the following still were using their swan marks: the Dukes of Norfolk, Richmond and Suffolk, the Earls of Essex, Oxford, Surrey and Sussex, the Bishops of Ely and Peterborough, King's and Jesus College, Cambridge.

Swans are extraordinarily long-lived. One died a year or two ago on the Thames at Windsor which was reputed to be over one hundred years old. A bird of this age would be very tough eating, but, in fact, all swans for the table have always been fed heavily and given the minimum of exercise so that it is no good going off to shoot any old swan which happens to be swimming about. Swans are now protected on most rivers, while on the Thames they are all privately owned either by the King, the Dyers Company or the Vintners Company.

The Dyers and Vintners mark their birds with certain incisions on the bill, whilst all unmarked birds belong to the King. Eton College used to own swans on the river, but they appear to have abandoned their rights on the annual journey up the Thames from Southwark Bridge to Henley by the swan master and his staff, known as swan upping.

During the Middle Ages, the swan was extremely expensive and was held in high esteem by the nobility. In fact such extortionate prices were charged that the City of London fixed a tariff of provisions in 1272 where swans were priced at three shillings and geese only twopence halfpenny. Peacock and swan appeared at almost every Royal banquet during the Middle Ages, often adorned with gold or silver foil or "flowered" with different coloured powders.

The mute swan (*Anus cyganus mansuetus*) is the swan which was generally used for food in England. It may measure three and a half feet in length, and often weighs 25 lb. The hen lays six to eight eggs and usually sits about 43 days, when the little grey cygnets leave the shell. During the early nineteenth century these eggs were often cooked.

In 1454 the swan was prepared in the following manner. The swan was first skewered into a sitting position. "Make a stiff bed of paste about the thickness of your thumb, colour it green, comb it out, and it will look like a meadow full of grass. Take your swan and gild him over with gold; then add a kind of loose flying coat of vermilion colour within, and painted with arms without, then set the swan upon his bed, cover some part of him with the cloak, stick about small banners on little sticks, the banners painted with the arms most agreeable to the persons seated at table." At a great banquet, on the eve of the Scottish Expedition, when two swans were brought in, accompanied by a flourish of trumpets, King Edward I vowed to avenge the murder of John Comyn and to punish Robert Bruce.

In 1419 the Brewers Company, for their annual feast, paid fifteen shillings for six swans, so prices may have fallen a little; by 1425 prices had fallen again as for another feast they paid three shillings and ninepence for 21 swans. In 1532 at a banquet by the Serjeants at Ely House, in honour of Henry VIII and Queen Catherine, 14 dozen swans were served. In 1575 swans were on a city tariff list at six to seven shillings each. Beaumont and Fletcher satirised the highly decorated type of cookery at these banquets by the following verse:

> "I'll make pigs speak French at table, and a fat swan
> Come sailing out of England with a challenge."

After the Restoration, the swan was very commonly served at Christmas Day dinners by the monied classes, although it was still comparatively expensive. It was not to become unfashionable with the nobility until turkeys began to make a frequent appearance during the reign of William III.

If you happen to have a spare swan about the place, the following recipe from 1725 is not recommended for trying out on your husband's managing director:

> "Skin and bone your swan, lard it with bacon, and season it with pepper, salt, cloves, mace and nutmeg to your palate and with a few bay leaves powdered; lay it in the pie; stick it with cloves; lay on butter and close the pie. When it is bak'd and half cold, fill it up with clarify'd butter."

The heavy seasoning was to kill the fishy flavour, but it is surprising that the swan is not boiled before being placed in the pie because if cooked using this recipe it would be as tough as leather, although the man who suggested it was chef to the Duke of Buckingham and to D'Aumont the French Ambassador.

> "Take 3 quarts of best vinegar, 1 quart of Lisbon wine, 3 large onions sliced, a handful of shallots, 4 bay leaves, some whole pepper, a little mace and cloves, and a handful of salt. Boil all together, put this pickle over your swan. It must lie twelve hours in the pickle. Then put it on to bake and baste your swan with the pickle."

Both these recipes are typical Restoration cookery; in fact, the type of dish to which Samuel Pepys was accustomed lingered on another hundred years with but little alteration.

Until recently, swans were prepared for the table in and around Norwich, and, unless it has been discontinued because of the war, the Corporation of Norwich still owns swans at St. Helens Swan Pit, and some cygnets were sold every Christmas at two guineas each. Cygnets were put to fatten on barley in August and they were allowed to eat as much food as possible until November. It was found inadvisable to keep them much later than November as they began to get tough and the flesh became very dark. A present of a Norwich cygnet was accompanied by the following recipe:

"Take three pounds of beef, beat fine in a mortar
Put it into the swan that is when you've got her.
Some pepper, salt, mace, some nutmeg, an onion
Will heighten the flavour in gourmand's opinion
Then tie it up tight with a small piece of tape
That the gravy and other things may not escape.
A meal paste, rather stiff, should be laid on the breast
And some whitened brown paper should cover the rest.
Fifteen minutes at least, ere the swan you take down
Pull the paste off the bird, that the breast may get brown."

The King has made a practice of presenting some of the Royal cygnets to the Mayor and Corporation of Windsor for their annual banquet. I believe these birds were specially fattened by the King's swan master.

J. F. HAMPTON

Sir, The old adage, Chacun à son goût, may cover a multiplicity of nastiness; but I believe that it may be laid down with some certainty that a swan of over twelve months old cannot be considered an inviting article of food in the twentieth century, let alone a delicacy. Indeed when a friend, staying here for the first time many years ago, was offered some Abbotsbury cygnet, he refused point-blank to make the experiment. He had recently, he said, been staying in one of the great houses of Norfolk, and had eaten swan, with the result that he had been very sick! The list of seasonings, mentioned by Mr. Hampton in his interesting article, may be cited as evidence to prove my contention.

The method by which cygnets at Abbotsbury have been prepared for the table for very many years is simplicity itself. They are taken up when a few days old, and are placed with a foster-mother, a hen swan, in open pens with small pools of water. For the first two or three months they are fed on chopped grass, and on a certain quantity of semi-marine weed, zostera and ruppia, which grow in the brackish waters of the Fleet nearby, the home of their parents.

Towards the end of August they are moved to a bigger pen, with spring water and a larger, though still quite small, pond. There they are fed largely on maize, with a certain modicum of the green foods cited above. To allow them to the open water, where they would feed chiefly on those weeds, would at once make the flesh fishy and rank. By the end of October they are quite fit to rear, and they continue tender until the following March or April.

No seasoning beyond a rich, brown sauce, or port wine pure and simple, is required. The best method of cooking is plain roast, either hot or cold. As feeding with grain has been impossible since the war, we this year tried feeding entirely on green food, with, as I feared, unsuccessful results.

The monks, to whom the swans belonged before the property passed by purchase into the possession of the Strangways family after the Reformation, apparently only marked their birds when destined for food. Marking came into use apparently in the seventeenth century. All swans at Abbotsbury are still marked – a nick with a penknife in the edge of the web of the foot when a few days old, which forms a V-shaped incision in later life. This is a painless and far less complicated proceeding than that practised on the Thames, which necessitates the handling of the almost full-grown bird.

Swans are traditionally believed to live 100 years, but I have never been able to trace any authentic instance of which real proof can be produced.

ILCHESTER

AN INTELLECTUAL
(1940)

The carp? Such a fish Walton, and all angling stylists call Water Fox. An alderman of a fish, scaled in gold and olive, his big fins richly and redly brown.

Where shall I take him? I see a lake, opulent with water-lilies, where the blue dragon-flies, in the August heat, go up and down as lances upon a foray. The lake lies in a deer park, beneath the four-square, noble House of Kimboling. Leave to fish for the monster carp here is not easy to obtain. Fortunately, His Grace's agent, young Lawley-Penrose, wants to marry my niece, so here I am, at 5 a.m., sat screened behind an upthrust of green bulrush on which rests a 10 ft. cane rod. Here I can see without being seen.

A small float lies idle in the empty channel between the lily beds. It buoys my bait, a new potato boiled in brown sugar, where, an hour since, I cast it out. I have pulled twenty yards of undressed silk line off my reel; they lie coiled within the lid of a large chocolate box (Lawley-Penrose says it with Charbonnel's best). A late brood of mallard scull by, quacking softly, the young birds as big as their mamma. So close they are that almost one might touch them. The sun comes tip-toe downhill among the old oak, and a dragon-fly, 5 inches of steel-blue, waking, poises upon a bulrush and sheers up and off into golden light.

A carp is a prodigious fighter but the big fish shall be drawn over the big net at last. And what now? I have little taste for taxidermy in the home, although, in heraldry, the carp is emblem of the utmost hospitality. I read that two hundred years is not old for a carp. Shall he then be cut off in his prime? Not by me. Presently I shall restore him to his lake. But first we will photograph him. Yes, the camera is at home; I am no optimist. I shall bicycle back for it and for a suitable reel, a matter of twenty minutes, half-an-hour at most. Meanwhile, Methuselah shall do well enough beneath a stack of wet bracken. A carp can live a long time out of water. He is in fact almost amphibious. (In Holland it is, I understand, customary to fatten carp for table by hanging the poor wretches in a net of wet moss and spoon feeding them, like babies, on bread and milk.)

But why, seeing that our carp is caught, do we want a reel other than this, my big one, here? The carp is not yet photographed and, well, the smaller the reel the bigger, by comparison, is the fish when the pair appear in company, an ornament to the piscatorial press.

PATRICK CHALMERS

ENCOUNTER WITH A CONGER
(1965)

Recently I came on a young conger eel in a rock pool. He was a small one and I let him slither away unmolested because I had no particular need of him alive or dead. He could not have been more than a pound in weight and, accidents barred, he had much growth to make, for he could easily end up as a 40- or 50- pounder and still fall far short of the British record.

A conger is not everybody's idea of a synonym for charm in the world of Nature, though I suppose that if one could make a sufficiently impersonal assessment one might admire such suppleness combined with such strength. But the bigger they get the less graceful they become, for their girth increases proportionately faster than their length and they lose their svelte figures.

At what poundage they acquire an ability to bark is not known, but perhaps they always have this intimidating talent, though only adults can do it loud enough to make themselves heard by human ears. Lest I be called a liar I must make it clear that I do not claim to have heard them baying at the moon, but so many people claim to have heard them bark that I accept the fact.

I have never caught a large conger and I have no wish to, for I gather from those who have that such are apt to get very rough in play. I base this belief on the tale of the eel-of-my-uncle, a true tale and not a bilingual exercise like the plume-of-my-jardinier.

He hired two Mauritians to take him out into deep water and in due course he hooked a vast eel. Apparently, the monster was more than obliging once it had been fought up to the boat, and skinned aboard with alacrity, where it proceeded to put a point of view with appalling vigour.

It raged around so savagely that it swiftly penned my uncle in the bows and the boatmen in the stern, where they conducted a Custer's-last-stand, backs-to-the-bulwarks type of defensive battle, banging it with oars and boathooks and making no great impression on it. My uncle said that only the fear of meeting the creature's twin stopped him from going overboard, but eventually it was persuaded to return to its element and a frightened boat's crew made all haste back to land.

I asked him how big it was, but he could only say that he had been too busy to measure it, and his impression was that it was about 20 ft. long with a head like a bull terrier at each end. Laying off a bit for wind, it might have been half that size, for a 12-footer has been taken in Australian waters and there are scientific grounds for thinking that far bigger ones exist.

Both conger and freshwater eels start life as curious little leaf-like transparencies which, when about 3 in. long, alter to become the miniature eels which we know as elvers, and then grow to maturity.

Link that fact to another and you get a startling conclusion. In the Marine Biological Laboratory at Charlottenlund, Denmark, is preserved just such a juvenile eel (or *leptocephalus*) which is slightly over 6 ft. long. If its adult size had borne the same ratio to its early dimensions as that of an ordinary eel it would have reached 60 ft. or 70 ft.

Perhaps they were correct as well as wise to bundle the eel-of-my-uncle overboard. No true sportsman keeps undersized fish.

C. C. L. BROWNE

THE PASSING WORLD OF UNCLE ARTHUR
(1969)

My Uncle Arthur's tale is that of thousands of other countrymen. But he has been a farmworker all his life; his years have spanned the change from the traditional methods, little altered over the centuries when man farmed by the physical efforts of himself and his horses, to the mighty mechanical beasts of today pulling four-furrow ploughs at a steady trot. Technology, besides transforming the countryside, has affected the lives of the men, and Arthur's life is the story of those farmers who experienced the upheaval.

Arthur was born the ninth, and last child of a Norfolk family who had been farmers as far back as they could recall. His education at the village school was rudimentary and finished at 13. Neither he nor his family considered any other work but the land and, even if they had, the prospects for a village boy in the towns were dismal. The arts of the farmworker came naturally to him, and so did the pursuit of the creatures of the countryside.

At the end of the First World War his elder brother bought a small farm in an isolated part of central Norfolk and Arthur went to work with him. It was 200 acres of heavy clay and if men ever hacked a living from the soil they did. As with most small farmers of the period, their activities covered almost everything – barley, sugarbeet, pigs, turkeys, chickens and a few dairy cows – and they worked seven days a week. Each morning after milking Arthur would turn to the land and his brother would chug off on his milk round with the rear of an old Austin filled with churns. I cannot recall their having a holiday, except for Christmas Day.

Times were hard for farmers in the twenties and, as the years moved into the thirties, they grew harder. Prices fell and, when the neighbouring farm entered the market, no-one would buy. The machinery went at the sale for a few shillings apiece, and then the men were gone and the buildings stood empty. Soon it was a jungle and we were the only visitors, gathering the walnuts each year from the big tree in the middle of a wilderness that had once been a fine lawn.

For more than 25 years they worked the little farm, and it was a form of slavery. Not only was the available machinery limited, but they could afford only the minimum. I recall one dry spring when the harrow could do nothing with the clods of baked clay; Arthur spent a fortnight wielding a sledgehammer in unbroken sunshine.

But at the heart of all the efforts were the horses – great, strong, docile creatures covered with clanking chains and vast leather collars with wisps of straw sticking out of the cracks. Hardly anything moved or worked without them. Theirs was

a leading part, from the time their breath spurted out like white mist in the cold autumn air as they strained the plough through the heavy land to the moment when the last load of the harvest rolled into the stackyard with the stars showing in an August sky.

There was no spraying and, while the fields grew poppies and thistles as well as corn, the horses worked lightly. But come July the binder would be pushed from the machine shed, the chicken droppings brushed off, the moving parts greased, and the harvest was at hand.

When the corn was ripe Arthur would scythe round the perimeter of the field, tying each sheaf with a wisp of straw; the binder would rattle through the gate drawn by the same pair of horses whose efforts had ploughed, harrowed, rolled and drilled the field.

We worked as few men work nowadays; although I was only a boy there were no spectators. We stopped when it was dark, having paused only for a few minutes at noon in the shadow of the hedge to eat cheese and sop from the bottle that had lain in the stream. As the strip of standing corn narrowed, so the rabbits began to bolt, and the sport was tremendous. Some were shot, some were run down in the long stubble, and others, thinking themselves unseen, slunk out to hide under the sheaves, only to be pinned by the weight of a heavy body.

When the shocks were dry, carting began; the horses knew the routine so well that they would pass down the line with the briefest of commands, turning right on the call of "weesh" and left on "cubee". Some time in the winter the threshing machine, drawn by the big steam engine, would arrive, and for a day or so all would be noise, dust and action. The stackyard would be surrounded by a fine-mesh wire fence to contain the rats and as the level sank, the sport increased.

The rats were everywhere. The large farms enjoyed some control by their gamekeepers, but the small ones had no time and accepted the rats as a part of life. With the cold they drew into the farm buildings and Arthur would shoot them at night with a .410 with a spotlight torch tied under the barrel. But they were too numerous to be controlled by random methods, and every winter each small farm would have its rat day. All the neighbours would arrive, by bicycle or elderly car, each with a small sack containing a ferret or two, and every piece of machinery or moveable cover would be dragged from the building. Up to a dozen ferrets would be popped into the maze of rat holes, a short pause would follow, and then bedlam commenced. There would be rats running across the floors, climbing the walls, along the gutters and even over the roof tiles. The squeals of cornered rats mingled with the cracks of .410s and garden guns and broad Norfolk voices having a day's fun. One of the wives would be in charge of first aid for ferrets which had fared badly, and she would be handed the wounded as they emerged. Eventually the sound of battle would fade, and the beer and sandwiches appear prior to putting everything back.

This was the background of Arthur's life – hard, simple and never varied except by the rhythm of the seasons. He accepted everything without comment or complaint, working slowly and deliberately but never pausing and never skimping a job. He exuded common sense as only a countryman who lives a wholly practical life can. I never heard him speak ill of anyone. I have known many more intelligent men, but none so endowed with reliability, industry and kindness. I never knew him visit the doctor or retire to bed ill, although he might feel unwell and rest in a dark corner of the farm.

His only real love was shooting. Each Sunday morning, after the cowshed had been washed down, he would set out with gun and dog. The gun was a nameless Belgian creation, bought for £6 10s and in use today. The dog was a spaniel who knew it was Sunday before anyone put a foot on the floor. To see the pair of them working stealthily down a hedge was a delight. Arthur could never lift a gun without assuming the manner of a poacher.

His eyes would flicker everywhere, seeking the rabbit in its form among the thistles, or the dot of a woodpigeon on the horizon, but always giving the impression of a man who expected the keeper to appear from nowhere. An old cloth cap rested on his ears, their edges frayed by constant exposure to freezing winds as he topped sugarbeet by hand or trimmed a hedge with a hook. He hunted in the true sense, without noise and with no fancy rules about giving the quarry a sporting chance. Much of the bag never even knew danger threatened before it died. The pigeon, thirsty from the corn stooks, gliding in to drink where the stream shallowed, would not notice the slight movement under the big oak, and a few seconds later would disappear into the sack slung across Arthur's back on an old leather strap.

He was never much good with the high fast shots, but at his own familiar targets he was deadly. The rabbit bursting across a gateway or the pheasant lifting over the hedge rarely escaped. Having killed, he would always gather up the loose feathers, pocket the empty cartridge case and move on. He believed that there was "no sense in letting the whole world know what you're about."

There was always a hutch of ferrets to be fed with bread and milk or a couple of still-warm sparrows. He had no time for good-natured ferrets which could be popped inside a man's shirt; he looked for strong, fierce creatures, which needed handling with respect and a strong leather glove. Mainly they were used for ratting, for there was little time for rabbiting and even less of a market in the rabbit-ridden Norfolk of pre-myxomatosis days.

The old farmhouse is derelict now, with the windows gone, and when I last made a visit to revive old memories an owl was in occupation. The garden seat where we sat on hot August nights and sang "Shine on harvest moon" is rotting and nearly swallowed by the once trimmed hedge. The land has changed with whole hedges swept away to create mammoth fields. The quiet uncultivated corners where the partridges nested, the little wood which the foxes favoured, the pond where I shot my first mallard with an air rifle – all under the plough. When the war had sent farm prices soaring my uncles sold, afraid that peace would bring a return to hard times, and it went, as is so often the case, to the largest adjoining owner. Arthur simply went to work on a nearby farm, riding to and fro from his cottage on an old bicycle, re-tyred countless times. He has never really accepted all the new farm machinery; he tolerates it, and is grateful for the effort it saves, but is, in his heart, a horse man.

The cough of a tractor engine bursting to life on a cold morning cannot be compared with the smells of a horse yard, nor diesel fumes with the smell of sweat from a pair of good horses pulling the plough against a rise in the land. When a man has little else in life, he forms a strong bond with his animals, and no mere lump of machinery can replace Dobbin with his gigantic legs, restless tail and great gentle eyes. There was always a Dobbin.

The horses have gone, and so in time will Arthur. He, and the others of his generation, are the last survivors of the old agriculture. Most of his working companions are younger men; friendly, hearty chaps but, with their tellies, small cars and Norwich every Saturday night, there is little common ground. Most were small children when the unemployment rate rose and the prices for farm produce fell, and some of them were unborn when the heavy bombers took off each night and crawled across a darkening velvet sky.

They have never backed a horse into the shafts of a cart, taken a cow to bull, searched a hedge for free-range eggs, served milk from a churn nor, deafened as they are by the roar of the tractor, heard the song of the plough through the soil. When Arthur and his generation have gone, an era will end and the countryside will be a less colourful and romantic place.

JOHN MARCHINGTON

ENGLISH AS SHE IS WRITTEN
(1930)

The printer is often ridiculed because of his errors, but all too often the scoffers forget that the printer is not always to blame.

Not long ago an Indian laundry proprietor circulated the soldiers and civilians of Noshera, advising them of the excellence of his establishment. His bill ran:

"Joyful Tidings.

"In Noshera there being as reliable source or an accurate firm for washing clothes etc. Dhobies treatment has been rather objectionable which the Gentlemen and Laidies giving them their clothes for washing purposes have been deeply feeling in getting backs their clothes neither preparing washed nor on the promised date and sometimes absolutely spoiled or lost. In order to remove all the gentlemen and Laidies disappointment in this respect we have started an up to date laundry situated at KB, Taj Mohammed Khan new building new Civil Boat bridge.

"It would as doubt be joyful tidings for all concerned that the foundation of the laundry is upon so on the and the aim of the firm is chiefly to work to the entire satisfaction of the public. The firm's employees are learnt specialists hence all work of washing, dry cleaning, dyning etc of all sorts of Silk, Woolen, Warm clothes, Blankets, Lungis, Rugs etc. etc. will be carried out with every satisfaction. To all this the firms charges will be very moderate which will entirely be left on the state of the work and the owners choice."

This is a fairly good notice and shows that the writer was not unacquainted with the intricacies of the English language. Others have fared less fortunately, as did the Japanese authorities when they once issued instructions to English motorists:

"At the rise of the hand of policeman stop rapidly. Do not pass him or otherwise disrespect him.

"When a passenger of the foot hove in sight tootle the horn trumpet to him melodiously at first. If he still obsticle your progress tootle him with vigour and express by word of mouth the warning 'Hi! Hi!'

"Beware of wandering horse that he shall not take fright as you pass him. Do not explode the exhaust box at him. Go soothingly by and stop by the roadside until he pass by.

"Give big space to the festive dog that makes sport in the highway. Avoid entanglement of dog with your spoke wheel.

"Go soothingly on the grease mud as there lurk the skid demon. Press the brake of the foot as you roll round the corners to save the collapse and tie up."

This Japanese notice is a curious mixture of dignified English and slang, but it certainly shows the possibilities of the language, and suggests what can be done with it.

ANON.

THE TWELFTH
(1936)

The north-bound expresses
Stand panting, impatient,
Awaiting the whistle,
The slam of their doors.
High in the roof hangs
The smoke of their engines,
Recalling the magic
Of cloud-haunted moors.

Out of the glittering
Turmoil of London,
Into the shadowy
Stretches of night,
Northward they thunder,
Relentless, untiring,
Through heather-dark ranges
In ribbons of light.

Forgotten the clamour,
The dust of the city;
We savour the sweetness
Of freedom begun:
The clear Northern morning
Shall greet us, returning,
Our feet in the heather,
Our hands on a gun

L. J. W.

September

WEATHER SIGNALS
(1936)

Sir, On the morning of a day's stalking, or a grouse drive, the guns, as a rule, ask the keeper in charge: "How about the weather?" Having acted in the capacity of head for a period of 30 years, I was considered a good judge, thanks to the following "nature signs" or signals, which I found most reliable:

If you're up with the lark at the dawn of new day,
Scan the clouds though afar in the air:
If they break up in patches, fading away,
That's a sure sign the day will keep fair.

But if small clouds drifting, or curling on high
Join on to dark cloud-banks, beware
Though the morning sun makes a faint break in the sky,
Remember the day won't keep fair.

If crows fly in circles and caw in the air,
And the morning dew dries on the heather,
Or if sheep start to gambol like lambs when at play,
These are three signs of raw, windy weather.

If the Red Deer trek down off the high mountain crest
Or the heath-clad side of the Ben,
While storm-clouds are gathering away in the west,
Then prepare for a hurricane.

GEORGE WILKIE

137

PARTRIDGES
(1924)

The partridge comes first. The grouse season opens earlier, of course, and some boys have the luck to begin their shooting days on the moors. But I think for most of us the shooting year begins with the day when we open the gate into the stubble-field – the First of September. That was the beginning for me, at all events, years before I was allowed to carry a gun. But the day when at last I was to walk after partridges, myself one of the guns – there is no day that comes back more vividly to me than that.

We used to be told in those days that the way to tell cock partridges from hens was to look at the breast feathers: if they carried a dark chestnut horseshoe the bird was a cock, and if not a hen. But that is only partially true. If in September you pick up a bird with a well-marked horseshoe, it is almost certainly a cock; but hens occasionally have horseshoes. The better test is to look at the median wing coverts: in the cock, these are marked with a longitudinal pale buff stripe running down the shaft, with grey or brown mottling either side of the shaft. In the hen there is the same pale buff stripe, but instead of the mottling there are buff and dark brown bars.

The English partridge's call is creaky, like screwed wood or metal – Tennyson writes of the partridge turning his "rusty key." But I always think its old English name "ptyryche" represents its call as nearly as any sound that can be put on paper – only by a coincidence, of course, for the name derives through French from the Latin.

There can be no question that driving partridge provides difficult shooting. Partridges driven late in the season on a windy day, when they are wild and wary and swerve at the sight of a gun, might be the most difficult shooting of all to be had in these islands. A driven grouse comes fast and he too can swerve, but his swerves are on a longer arc. He is not so incalculable as the partridge.

The temptation for a beginner is "browning" a covey, or firing in a vague and general way at what appears to be a thick bunch of birds of which you think you cannot help hitting one. A driven covey sweeps over the fence at such a pace, and apparently so close together that the beginner thinks he will have no time to pick a single bird, and fires into the middle of the covey. Having done so, he finds almost invariably that the covey flies on without a feather being touched, or worse, that a bird flinches slightly, but gets away with the rest. But the birds are not really very close together. There are spaces of cubic yards of air between them, and it is into those spaces that you shoot. If you do not look at an individual bird as you pull the trigger, what you will do is to pick an empty space and fire at blank air. Shooting driven partridges is like playing first-class bowling: each oncoming bird, like each approaching ball, is different, and you have to decide in a moment how to deal with it, with your brain, your arms and your feet working perfectly together.

But, with all the fascination of the difficulty of driven partridges, I prefer walking them up. In driving you go to your stand and you stay there. You may have a wonderful stretch of country before you – the breckland of Norfolk, perhaps, or the blue distances of Salisbury Plain – but you cannot afford to think long or much of what lies beyond the fence, for you must be watching for what is to come over.

In walking you have time for everything you want to do. I like the early September morning: the dew is grey on the grass of the lawn and the zinnias in the border. I like walking to the first gate, and thinking that for the first time I am going to tread the crumbled soil between the swedes and feel the little pools of rain pour from the leaves on my boots. I like the flowers and fruit in the hedges; the travellers' joy turning to old man's beard, the bryony twining red and green and yellow on the hazel, the blackberries hot and vinous in the sun. I like hearing the bees humming over acres of mustard, and smelling the honey in the clover. The clover, too, holds butterflies – painted ladies darting about, brimstones dancing down the hedgerow and swallows hawking after them – you can hear the snap of the beak – and clouded yellows, the butterflies I love best of all, swaying on the warm blossoms. When is the world a happier place?

PATRICK CHALMERS

OF MEN, MICE AND ONIONS
(1971)

A brilliant man can, I fancy, assess current facts correctly and from them deduce future events, whereas a clever man can arrive at the latter only by starting from established data. Some of us get the data but deduce precious little therefrom; others do not even notice what is happening under their noses.

I was once a guest at a business man's shoot and nobody had a drink at luncheon until he had rung up the City. He returned saying that all was quiet and Ford's had moved one sixteenth, and everybody sighed with relief except me who did not know what game was being played, let alone the score in it. That was an example of hearing something but being unable to relate it to the future.

At this moment, I possess certain facts and can deduce little from them. In the spring I planted 80 yards of onions because I like the look of the crop, and I have just finished lifting them. Had they been a pack of hounds, "level" is not the adjective that would occur to one because they ranged in size from mini-coconuts to maxi-peas, and I was puzzled until I realized that the ground was honeycombed with mouse-burrows. Six times in 10 yards, when I pulled up an onion a mouse dashed from its disturbed home to take cover in the neighbouring savoys.

It was not so much that they had nibbled the crop as that they had undermined it, leaving many onions dangling their roots into tunnels after the manner of vegetable chandeliers, and such had not prospered. Only those whose roots were firmly in the earth had come to full stature. It does not matter because we have more than we can use this winter; but the point is that much the same would seem to apply to the mice.

What eludes me is the appropriate action to take about this superabundance. A woman might insist that we swiftly dig a moat around the house. A go-getting tycoon might try to corner the nation's stock of mouse-traps. A doctor might advocate inoculation against something-or-other. An ornithologist might forecast a plethora of owls.

A cats'-meat merchant might cancel his contracts with the knacker, certain that owners would find their pets were living comfortably off the land and that his trade was about to hit a recession. But I am not a female doctor who likes birds and indulges in trade on the side, and none of these possible courses of action appeals.

When one is faced with an ill-defined problem, one can sometimes resolve it by exploring extremes. I have covered various positive actions and there remains to brood over masterly inactivity. Now Nature abhors a superfluity no less than She does a vacuum and, given time, will organise predators, lack of food, disease, a hysterical migratory urge or such disaster to relieve pressure.

It may take time though, and perhaps one should assess the damage-potential to crops of a multitude of mice. I no longer grow their favourite Wedgwood iris and, though we plant some peas for ourselves, it will be months before the mice can get at them and they may have been decimated by then. In fact, there is nothing very vulnerable and it seems sense to do nothing very earnest.

Unwittingly I may have imported a control already. The other day I collected one Chinese gentleman and two Chinese ladies to keep the grass short in the paddock-half of the walled-garden. From the way the gander worried my finger when I was freeing him from his sack, a mouse would be well-advised to give him a wide berth. I sense a pot-pourri of disasters building up against the mice and they seem due for a culling. If it happens this winter, I may yet grow a uniform crop of onions next year.

C. C. L. BROWNE

Sir, I must express my interest and appreciation of Brigadier C. C. L. Browne's detailed description of the ravages by rodents in his onion garden. My experience with the liquidation of rodents may instil a thought in his mind to follow the Biblical dictum: Go Thou And Do Likewise.

Some years ago I had a 200 acre farm in the State of Utah, America, on which I had a print shop as a hobby. One day I opened a drawer and found a nest in one of the compartments with a large fat mouse nursing 10 hairless mice "pups."

I picked her up by the tail and, with her progeny firmly entrenched to her mild taps, I flung her out of the back door.

My research in the cause of erosion of the cement floor in Cola bottling plants came in handy. I took a bottle of unfinished Cola and poured half in one saucer and half in another. I then placed each saucer at one end of the shop. The next morning I found four dead mice and two dead rats on the floor. I do not know if any or how many died outside.

The regular mouse traps never paid dividends. But the phosphoric acid and sugar in the Cola did the work.

N. W. WALKER (ARIZONA, U.S.A.)

A KESTREL IN THE FAMILY
(1972)

One Friday early in August the telephone rang. Someone had found an injured kestrel, and we decided to take her on. We collected her in a fishing basket and brought her home. She was in poor shape; the couple who had found her admitted that they did not know how to feed her. Her legs were unsteady and although her eyes were bright, she had little appetite. We put her on a block in the work-shop, but she was unable to stand and had badly fouled tail feathers. Early next morning my 13-year-old son, Jonathan, reported that she was no better. Fortunately it was the beginning of the school holidays, so he and his sister, Lorna, were able to devote their time looking after her. We decided to call her Jasmine.

She was fed regularly throughout the first day, but she ate little and became increasingly weak. A vet was consulted. He thought she might be suffering from malnutrition or toxic chemicals and doubted if she would survive. That night she was too weak to perch on the block so we put her on a piece of old blanket in Jonathan's fishing creel. On Sunday morning she was alive, but only just. Hot-water bottles were filled throughout the day to help her almost paralysed legs.

She was forcibly fed, my husband pushing small pieces of best beef steak down her unwilling gullet while Jonathan held her. She was too weak to struggle much. We offered her water, knowing that only a very sick kestrel will drink in captivity, but she drank greedily each time water was offered. Sometimes we added a few drops of brandy. We moved her basket round the workshop so that she was never out of the sun.

On Monday we could see a slight improvement. For a week we fed her, gave her water and tried to inspire in her a will to live. Gradually she improved and began to preen herself, but she still sat on her haunches rather than supporting herself on her claws. My husband suggested that if we put jesses on her it might take her mind off her illness. So slim leather straps were fitted to each leg and the therapy appeared to work. She pecked at the straps and soon began to feed herself and to fly about the workshop. Her shed was scrubbed daily with disinfectant and she was taken for rides in the car so that she had to grip the front seat in order to strengthen her claws.

For two months Jasmine ruled our lives. Local children brought her mice which she would stretch out and then swallow in one gulp. But we had to face the fact that ultimately she would be released. She was a wild creature and must be returned to the fields and woods.

Our house stands on a ridge commanding a wide sweep of farmland to the river below with an uninterrupted view for a mile or more. It was in the field in front of our house that her training began. With Jasmine on a long line, Jonathan would hold her on a gloved hand; my husband would then whistle and at the same time throw the lure, which we had made of pigeon feathers. She was released and would fly high and then stoop to the lure when we would pick her up and feed her by hand.

We repeated this performance about three times every evening. Soon she was flying free. Each day we would set her block on the lawn in the shade and, at our approach, she would chatter like an excited monkey.

One Sunday morning we saw another kestrel on telephone wires nearby. This seemed the ideal time to give Jasmine her freedom. We fetched her from the workshop with heavy hearts, said our farewells and cast her up into the air. She saw the other kestrel, who was now mobbing a crow, and through our binoculars we watched her. She still had her jesses on; we were thrilled to see that it was Jasmine who flew higher, who swooped faster and who was generally the fitter of the two. Tiring of the sport, she flew away from the other kestrel and the crow until she was a speck in the distance.

We thought she had gone out of our lives forever. We worried in case her jesses tangled in a tree. We knew that one toe was deformed and would never be right. We wished we had kept her just a week longer, made sure she was strong enough to fend for herself. We whistled, swung the lure and from out of the blue came a tiny speck. Again the whistle, again the whirling lure and, from a great height, chattering like a magpie Jasmine stooped to the lure. Quickly Jonathan took her on the glove and fed her.

We removed her jesses and my husband continued to whistle for her at the same time for another 10 days; then one evening she did not come back and we never saw her again. She had returned to the wild.

SUSAN I. HATTON

TAME BIRDS
(1920)

Sir, On Bank Holiday (August 2) I picked up a young swift (Cypselus apus) which had apparently fallen from its nest in fledgling condition. The left wing had been injured, and the lower mandible was bent in such a way as to prevent it from feeding.

For the last thirty days I have carefully nursed it, and fed it on finely-shredded raw and cooked meat every three hours, housing it in the meantime in a ventilated cardboard-box lined with flannel. I give it water on the tip of my finger. When placed on the ground or lawn it struggles back to me, and is never happier than when nestling in my half-closed hand. Its favourite position is inside the kitchen fender, close to the range, the warmth of which is a special attraction, and on hearing my voice it intelligently turns round and flutters towards me. My only fear is that my protégé may not survive the winter, and that its inability (so far) to fly may react on its constitution.

I do not suppose that this case is an isolated one, and I should be glad to have any information calculated to ensure its survival.

(MRS.) CARDIGAN WILLIAMS

[Cooked meat should on no account be given, being so indigestible that even to such a large birds as hawks and owls it has proved fatal if continued. – The Editor.]

(1902)

Sir, A bullfinch which I caught in a gooseberry net in August last, a young bird that could hardly peck up, is now very tame, and comes out of the cage every day, perching on my arm when held up for him at an angle. The moment he hears the water running from the tap into the sink, he is there to have a wash, which he seems to enjoy very much. But, more remarkable still, he talks quite plain, as plain as a parrot, and as my occupation only allows me in my rooms at meal times, the bird repeats all he knows to me as he has picked it up in rotation. When I enter the room and go close to his cage, after he has said all he has to say I let him out, and after he has had a five minutes tugging at the mat, he will come on my arm and seems delighted to repeat his little knowledge to me; he will also let me handle him and is not the least shy. He is, in fact, a unique bullfinch, and I should like to know what would be the value of such a bird.

W. KENT

(1895)

Sir, The great difficulty in rearing young swallows is the supply of proper food. Some beekeepers maintain that swallows take bees, but I never saw them do so; however the idea struck me that, if true, I would see if it were possible to rear some young ones on bees.

Accordingly, I took a nest of five fully-fledged barn swallows (hirondo rustica) and put them to the test. They were the second brood, and as it was during harvest time I was naturally up in good

*time every morning. I then got about a cup full of bees from the hive
for a start, and, of course had to kill them to keep them in the cup. I
then reduced them to a fine pulp with a pestle. With this I fed the
birds all round with a quill. After the first two days this was no
trouble, as they would open their beaks quite naturally and swallow
what was offered them. This was repeated every half-hour. The first
supply of bees would last till about 1 p.m., when a fresh supply was
obtained, and the process repeated till 10 p.m. . . .*

*I have now no doubt that the birds died of indigestion and
starvation combined. From subsequent observation I found that the
interval between meals served by parent birds was rather different
from mine – viz. three and a half minutes. From several timings on
different days I found that the average interval, taking the two old
birds together, was about forty-five seconds. . . . This goes on all
summer, from daylight to dusk, so that the quantity of insects
destroyed by a single pair of swallows must be something enormous.
It would take two persons at least to feed a single brood under
conditions at approaching nature. As to the number of bees per day, I
can only say it reduced a fairly strong stock quite perceptibly.*

ROBERT TOD

MR. PIMPKIN OBLIGES
(1942)

If your garden is just too small for a full-time gardener and
just too large to be kept clean by your own hands, then you
will fall victim, sooner or later, to the jobbing gardener. You
first find him in the advertisement columns of the local
newspaper, and it appears from the wording of the
advertisement that he is practically in distress. "Two or three
days a week urgently wanted. Any time. Anywhere." So you
rush off to him at the first opportunity, knowing how
difficult gardeners are to get in war-time, and find yourself
confronted at the cottage door by his wife, who puts her nose
round the door and says "Well?" and then, when you explain,
says he's had practically the whole neighbourhood round that

morning bothering him to go here and go there and he don't for the life of him know what to do he's got too much on hand already but anyway what name is it he'll very likely come round when he's had his tea.

You forget to point out the odd state of things by which a man who already has too much work is forced to waste money advertising for more, and you go home and wait for him to come. You wait there all evening, with the depressing feeling that he is conferring an immense favour on you by even considering your name, and in the end, of course, he does not come. He does not come, in fact, within the next ten days, and you begin to get desperate.

Spring is now coming on; the onions are not in; the borders are not forked; the rambler roses have not been tied. Finally you can wait no longer and you decide in desperation on an advertisement of your own. You draft this out with great care and take it into the offices of the local newspaper. It will appear the following day. That evening, in the middle of supper (it is always in the middle of a meal) the maid comes in and says, excuse her please but it is Mr. Pimpkin. You cannot for the life of you remember anyone named Pimpkin but you leave your mutton chop to get cold and go to the kitchen door, and there, looking as pleasant as if he came straight from the undertakers, is Mr. Pimpkin. You say good-evening, not having the slightest idea who he is, and he says: "I couldn't come afore. I ent bin well."

He does, in fact, look rather cadaverous and is obviously, in the language of the films, a sour-puss. He is about 63, with legs like scythe-handles, and he seems to be wearing three suits, of which he has the brown trousers of one, the blue waistcoat of another and the black jacket of the third. He wears a stiff collar without a tie, and his Adam's apple lodges on it like the butt of a pump handle.

As he offers no further explanation of his presence you say "you are very sorry he ent bin well," and he says: "Yis it gives me such jee-up every few weeks. I've ad it this twelve-month or more. Course I were in there nigh on a twelve-month."

"You were?" you say, and he says: "Yis! Twelve month all but three weeks," as if he is rather pained that you are unfamiliar with this private and mysterious phase of his history.

You keep silence, sympathetically, and then he warms up. You ought of course to have been prepared, but you are not: "Ad over three hundred injections."

"Did you indeed?"

"Ah. Course I were in there a twelve-month."

"Tut-tut," you say and then, because after it would be nice to touch at least the fringe of the subject in hand, you remark that you expect he is getting about a bit now. "Yis, but I hadn't ought to!" he says. "I ent right, y'know. I ent right."

"It's been a tough winter for everybody," you say.

"Ah!" he says. He puts into his voice a hint of vindictiveness. "Some ave bin all right. Some ent done bad. Some as I know. I tell you."

By this time the grease has grown white and cold on your mutton chop, or the remains of it have been burnt to a cinder under the grill, and the situation needs a piece of desperate brutality. "Well, Mr. Pimpkin," you say, "I've got an appointment in ten minutes. How many days a week do you think you can come?"

"Well," he says with absolutely funereal fatalism, "I han't ought to come at all be rights."

"Oh?"

"Be right," he says, "I han't ought."

"Oh."

"I've ad so many arter me."

"Well, do you think you could come two days? Two and a half days?"

"Well," he says, "I shall etta see. I shall etta see what I can do for you. I shall etta see if I can fit y'in Thursdays an Saturdays."

All right, you tell him, you'll leave it like that, and he'll etta see. The notion that he is conferring an immense favour on you has by this time increased enormously, and you yourself do not care any longer whether he comes or not. But you are a civil person, and it has been a charming Spring day and you politely mention this fact as you say good-evening and he goes down the garden path. "Ah!" he says, "too nice! We shall etta suffer for it! You see. It ent seasonable. We shall etta suffer!"

Finally he goes, and you go back to a mutton chop that has lost its identity. You have given up caring now whether he comes or not and you console yourself that you have after all put in an advertisement of your own.

Unfortunately there are no replies from your own advertisement, and you are forced back on the hope that Mr. Pimpkin will come. And finally, all in his own good time, at leisure, at the curious hour of twenty minutes past nine on Thursday morning, he comes.

It is a very nice morning; larks are singing over the ploughed land; sparrows are pecking the sweet polyanthus buds. You can smell Spring in the air and it is time to sow onions. You have a well prepared bed under a south wall, and it is there, by early sowing, that you raise early vegetables. You point out to Mr. Pimpkin that you think it would be an excellent thing to sow a few rows of early carrots, onions and peas in this bed, and you give him the seeds. He ignores them utterly. "I ent got mine in," he says.

"I'm all for early sowing," you say.

"Ah! but you don't want to be in 'urry," he says.

"I'm all for early sowing," you say. "This is an early garden. We're always early."

"That rose oughta bin tied up," he says.

You agree that the rose oughta bin tied up and perhaps he will do it during the day? You also want the peas, carrots and onions sown, and will he clear the next piece of ground of Brussels sprouts, which have gone over? "You don't wanta git them up," he says.

"They're finished," you say. "They're simply using good ground."

"I ent got mine up," he says.

This being final, you walk away. Mr. Pimpkin ent got his up, so you don't get yours up. The sooner you realise that the better.

Forty minutes later you come out into the garden to see if Mr. Pimpkin is anywhere to be seen. No seeds have been sown, no rows drawn. There are signs that the rose has been pruned, but Mr. Pimpkin himself has vanished. You walk up and down the garden several times and then finally, by chance, you see Mr. Pimpkin.

He is sitting in the greenhouse. It is very warm and sunny
in the greenhouse, and Mr. Pimpkin is sitting on a box. The
Daily Mail is spread on his knees, and on the *Daily Mail* is
spread a mountainous sandwich of bread and cheese, a couple
of slices of bacon and a large Thermos flask of tea. Mr.
Pimpkin is slowly masticating his way through both the news
and the food. You go into the greenhouse, struck instantly by
its soft and genial warmth, to remark to Mr. Pimpkin hullo
this is where he is. "Jist evvin me breakfast," he says.

You are wondering why Mr. Pimpkin cannot have his
breakfast, as other people do, in his own home and in his
own time, when the problem is solved for you. "Ent bin able
to git nothing down fust thing since I were bad."

"Oh."

"I ent arf th' eater I were," Mr. Pimpkin says. "Missus
used to say she wondered wheer I put it all."

As Mr. Pimpkin is about to overload his stomach with a
hunk of bread and cheese weighing about a quarter of a
pound, which at any moment he will wash down with a pint
of tea, you too are inclined to wonder where he puts it all.
"Ent you got no heat in your greenhouse?" he finally says.

You apologise for the lack of heating in the greenhouse,
which is only eight by fifteen, although you cannot help
noticing at the same time that Mr. Pimpkin looks as warm as
toast. You point out that it is really only a little place for
raising seeds, at which Mr. Pimpkin, who appears already to
have spent twenty minutes or more on his breakfast, begins
an expansive reminiscence on the wonderful greenhouses of
Lord Blather of Shotover, for whom he worked, man and
boy, for 30 years. This reminiscence is like a river with
countless tributaries. At each tributary Mr. Pimpkin branches
off to tell either the story of the under-butler who carried on
a long and foul intrigue about the chickens kept by Mr.
Pimpkin for Lord Blather in 1902, or the story of Lord
Blather's son who misled a parlourmaid in 1906 and two
housemaids in 1907 and against whom, for some dark reason,
Mr. Pimpkin still nurses an indissoluble hatred.

These tributaries have backwaters, and Mr. Pimpkin,
exploring them all, does so on the supposition that you are as

familiar with Lord Blather's lineage and property, his servants and their intrigues, their families and antecedents, as Mr. Pimpkin himself. These explorations take half an hour, by which time Mr. Pimpkin condescends to return to the main theme, the whole point of which is that Lord Blather suffered with his kidneys and did not like cucumbers. Having presented you with this tremendous information Mr. Pimpkin screws down his Thermos flask and says: "Well, I suppose we'd better git on afore we ev dinner-time on top of us."

Dinner-time is, in fact, on top of us before you know anything at all. Mr. Pimpkin again sits in the greenhouse to have his dinner, and at one-thirty, when you go in there to look at the petunia seedlings, you discover that the place has been fumigated by Mr. Pimpkin's pipe, in which he smokes a species of shag that smells like a combination of burning horse-hooves and dung. Outside, Mr. Pimpkin is calmly clipping the lonicera hedge. You suppress your annoyance and ask why the hedge takes preference over the onions, still not sown! "Oughta bin done afore," Mr. Pimpkin says.

This is final. Nothing can get past it. As the weeks go past you are to discover painfully that the garden is full of jobs that oughta bin done afore and that Mr. Pimpkin will, regardless of whatever you say, do them.

After this, having been caught in the morning by the private history of Lord Blather, you retire as far from Mr. Pimpkin as possible in the belief that Mr. Pimpkin works better in solitude. At three o'clock you come back to the lonicera hedge, which divides the garden from the field beyond, only to discover Mr. Pimpkin sharing a pipeful of shag with Charley, the horse-keeper from the farm, who is supposed to be chain-harrowing the pasture.

You hear Charley say that it feels like rain, and Mr. Pimpkin earnestly agrees he is right. You get the impression that Mr. Pimpkin would be extremely glad if it did rain, and you seize a hoe and begin to make loud and angry noises on the plot by the wall. Ten minutes later Mr. Pimpkin condescends to exchange heavy farewells with Charley, as if both were going to the ends of the earth. "Well, mind ow you goo on," he says, and Charley says "Ah!" and "gee-up" to the horses. Mr. Pimpkin then strikes practically a dozen matches, gives as many spits, and finally proceeds to clip the hedge in a cloud of evil fog.

You yourself work hard on the seed-drills for the rest of the afternoon, and at four-thirty you go to the house for a hasty cup of tea. At a quarter to five you go to find Mr. Pimpkin again to ask him for the seeds, only to find that Mr. Pimpkin has gone home, taking the seeds in his pocket.

He continues to come all summer. Your first real shock is when you pay him at the end of the first week. The local rate used to be a shilling an hour, but it has risen to one and a penny. When you ask Mr. Pimpkin how much, he says "I got it down somewheres" and forages in his pocket for a dirty scrap of paper from which falls a shower of shag. "Semteen hours at one an four I mak it," he says, "an you goo arves wi' Miss Ratcliffe on insurance."

You are about to protest at this monstrous statement when you remember that one of your pet hopes about the countryside is higher wages for country workers, and who are you not to set an example? Of Miss Ratcliffe you have never heard, and you can only wonder how it is you should halve the burden of insurance with her when she employs Mr. Pimpkin for four days and you for two.

Mr. Pimpkin continues to confer the favour of his presence on you, weather and health permitting, every Thursday and Saturday. Sometimes it rains; sometimes it's me back giving me gee-up again; sometimes Miss Ratcliffe dint gie me no peace till I went and done that cesspool job. Miss Ratcliffe emerges as a tyrant. If Mr. Pimpkin dominates you, Miss Ratcliffe dominates Mr. Pimpkin. Though he leaves you promptly at five forty-five, he apparently works without protest for Miss Ratcliffe until seven-thirty. He protests that March is too early for planting potatoes, but in April, when you finally plant them, it appears that Miss Ratcliffe ad ern in three weeks agoo. Your onions, which you eventually sowed yourself, germinate magnificently; but you ought to see Miss Ratcliffe's. Miss Ratcliffe is always referred to as She. You suggest that Mr. Pimpkin should sow French beans in boxes, but Mr. Pimpkin is against it: She never does. You suggest planting out the celery, but Good God no, She aint got ern out yet. Doesn't Mr. Pimpkin think the tulips are good? He does; but She's got a bed of tulips Mr. Pimpkin planted and you never see nothing like it. Shouldn't we grow summer cabbage? Well, Mr. Pimpkin says, you do what you like, but She never does. In the end, oppressed either by what Miss Ratcliffe does so excellently and what she doesn't do at all, you have a violent desire to wring Miss Ratcliffe's neck.

All through the summer Miss Ratcliffe, Lord Blather, the butler who intrigued against Mr. Pimpkin and, above all, the hospital are Mr. Pimpkin's dominating themes. If you ask him if he thinks it advisable to thin the peaches he goes back to the year 1903 when, it appears, the peaches at Lord Blather's were as large as pumpkins. If you complain of a cold in the head he will instantly draw your attention to the acute sufferings of stone on the kidney and layin on me back for a twelve-month. In short, nothing you do is so good, so bad, so successful or so painful as the things done by Miss Ratcliffe, Lord Blather, and Mr. Pimpkin.

Apart from the fact that he never does as he is told, always clipping the hedge when you want seeds sown, always tying roses when you want the lawn cut, Mr. Pimpkin has certain favourite horticultural pastimes. One of these is the process of settin back. Most of your cherished shrubs, roses and perennials, it seems, want settin back: the art is to seize secateurs and shears and cut the most flourishing species of the garden to the ground. Anything growing with unusually healthy vigour wants setting back. Mr. Pimpkin adores this pastime; whenever your back is turned he tries it out on the forsythia, the ceanothus, the philadelphus, the flowering currant, the buddleia, the southernwood and the rest.

You come into the garden to regard with horror some treasured shrub cut to the ground. "Ah! but you wun arf see a difference," Mr. Pimpkin says: than which, of course, there is no truer word. You certainly do see a difference. Unfortunately the forsythia and the philadelphus have been cut at the wrong season and will not now, flower for two years. The buddleia is the summer variety and not the autumn variety and will not flower for two years either. The flowering currant is indestructible anyway, but the ceanothus and the southernwood die in the winter. Certainly you don't arf see a difference in things.

All this time Mr. Pimpkin succeeds in making you feel that he is continually conferring an immense favour on you; that you are a horticultural ignoramus; that your garden and all it contains are quite beneath comparison with those of the best people; and that at any moment he will have to withdraw his patronage. "I ev a job to fit in everybody now," he says, "And She keep a-bothering me to go full time." All this appears to come rather strangely from a man who, only a month or two ago, was begging by advertisement for extra work, but you let it pass.

From this time onward Mr. Pimpkin's hours become increasingly erratic. He arrives at ten past nine and leaves at five to twelve; he arrives at one twenty and knocks off at five. He comes for only a day and a half, then a day, and finally half a day a week. By the time he has lit his pipe thirty times, ad me mite o' breakfast and set back the *Rosa Moyseii*, which in consequence is reduced to nothing, it is time to go home.

Finally there arrives a week when Mr. Pimpkin does not come at all. You can hardly believe this, and you wait another week for confirmation. Mr. Pimpkin still does not come, and the next day you hear, by means of the village Gestapo, that Mr. Pimpkin is working for Miss Ratcliffe full time.

On the day you hear that announcement you go out into the garden. You walk up and down. The air is free of shag, and in the greenhouse Mr. Pimpkin, who ent arf th' eater he were, is no longer trying to get down enough food for a cart horse. There is no Lord Blather, no butler, no Miss Ratcliffe. But this is not all. There is another difference. It is more subtle; it seems to be part of yourself and you cannot define it.

For a long time you cannot understand what it is or why if affects you as it does. Then suddenly you do understand. You realise that the garden is your own; it belongs not to Mr. Pimpkin any longer, but to you; at last you can do what you like with it and not as Mr. Pimpkin says you must do.

And for the first time in several months you are happy.

H. E. BATES

ON MEMORY'S MOUNT
(1936)

On Memory's mount I cross the seas;
I could not ask a stouter steed;
A better horse between my knees
    I'll never need.

For when he reaches at the rein
And plunges like a colt at play.
He takes me to a Bushland plain
    A world away.

He carries me the timber through,
With never touch against a tree,
On blind ways where the Brumbies flew
    In 'Ninety-three.

He takes me to the cattle-camp
Where, riding round five hundred head.
We heard the restless pikers tramp
    With ceaseless tread.

And he can take me back once more
To stockyard-rails and corral-wings,
To saddle-block and station store,
    And old loved things.

And so I live remembered days
When blood ran swift and hope ran high
On wide untrodden Western ways
    Beneath blue sky.

I ride him till he flings the foam;
I could not ask a better hack;
He knows the fields where I would roam,
    And takes me back!

WILL H. OGILVIE

October

GROUSE FOR DINNER
(1942)

Sir, Recently I decided I would go up to a far distant allotment of mine here in search of a brace of grouse.

The weather being unsuitable, I decided to give it up and went to look for mushrooms instead on low ground far from the moors. Here grouse are rarely seen, except in abnormally cold winter weather when they are unable to obtain food in their natural surroundings, owing to seep frozen snow.

Imagine my surprise, therefore, when I suddenly came upon a grouse. The bird seemed somewhat bewildered, ran in front of me a short distance, then got up and flew, low and straight, into a five-barred gate.

The bird was completely stunned and I went up and soon bagged it. Without the use of a gun, I had secured my grouse for dinner.

Trevor Thornton-Berry

A CZECH AT THE SHOOT
(1943)

"Come along, you lazy devil, I'll take you to a shooting party" said Doctor Boswell, "They are quite different from shooting parties in your country." He turned his pipe bowl downwards and looked at me over the top of his glasses, "I say you won't have seen anything like it in your life," he said with emphasis.

The next morning the good doctor slung round my neck a haversack full of cartridges, and thrust into my hand a case with food. "That's how it's done," he said. Instead of a gun he put a stick into my hand. It was said to make a good seat. My later experience showed me that it was also able to sink into the hopeless English mud.

"This is how one dresses oneself for a shooting party. Look at me." I looked and I saw. In the place of the respectable English doctor there stood before me what I should have taken for a tramp. With a funny hat he wore a shabby jacket and short, boyish trousers and, believe me or not, in contrast with all that, his gumboots were so shining and new they looked as if they had just been stolen. "Really! I have never seen anything like it in my life," I remarked in surprise.

"Nonsense," he answered. "You haven't seen anything. I am not properly dressed yet." The doctor took from the sack what at first looked like the leg of a pair of trousers and then something which seemed to be a sack to which leaves were sewn. "This is to protect me against the rain," he said. The trousers were too short, the sleeves too long, and the whole of the dress looked as if it were meant for a scarecrow. "Nice, isn't it?" "Beautiful," I answered, deeply moved. "Very beautiful."

We got into a car which was so small that I had not enough room to stretch my legs. The strap of the shooting bag cut deeply into my neck, and the case with the food pressed so hard on my tummy that my eyes nearly popped out of my head. The doctor driving the car puffed the smoke of his pipe into my eyes.

We drove seven miles, until we stood before a fairy-tale castle, or, if you would prefer a more modern comparison, a film castle. "Here we are," said the doctor and jumped out of the car. I looked in ecstasy at the red turret with the black clock, at the park in which the castle stood and at all the beauty which loomed up so suddenly before me. "Come on, come on," called Dr. Boswell. "I have to introduce you."

In the middle of the courtyard stood five tramps. The good doctor looked almost a dandy in comparison.

"This is my Czech, a lazy devil," was his form of introduction. He tried to persuade me that these tramps were Lord S., Commodore P., Lord D., and Colonel A. – I especially liked Lord S. He was wearing a pair of trousers several inches shorter than the doctor's, although he was quite a foot taller. The Commodore looked like a butcher and, later on, when we became better acquainted, I discovered he could swear like a trooper. I was, at that moment, obliged to compare all this with my pre-war imagination of what an English Lord was like, with my images of immaculately dressed gentlemen, with cold, stern faces.

We drove through fields and meadows. The rain was pouring down. No one seemed to notice the weather, no one grumbled about it. I would like to have joined someone in a good hearty grumble, especially when my shoes began to fill with water. But the party were laughing at the witty remarks of the Commodore. He talked about everything, but, alas, he did not say anything about himself. For example, he did not mention how big was his ship, or any of the brave deeds with which he certainly must have distinguished himself – nothing at all, absolutely nothing.

We formed a line as we were about to attack. I remained always with the good doctor, the haversack still slung round my neck. "Lord S. wants to preserve the hens, so we must not shoot them. I can't see well, so look out whether it is a hen or a cock and shout in time," ordered Dr. Boswell.

The beaters had already begun their work. They advanced across the turnip field towards us, shouting much more than their two bob's worth. They beat with sticks everything they could. But when not so much as a sparrow flew up, they began to flatter the pheasants, as in politics: "Come on, boys, come on, be good, sh, sh, sh." But the pheasants seemed to dislike the rain and preferred not to show themselves. However, at last, two flew up. "What is it? What is it?" shouted the doctor. "Pheasants," I replied.

"You silly ass. Are they cocks or hens?" he asked desperately. "Cocks," I answered haphazardly. Dr. Boswell pulled both triggers of his gun. Believe me or not, he hit his target. A pheasant came down like a stone. "I've got him! I've got him!" shouted the doctor excitedly.

"You've got *her*, Bozzy," corrected a fellow shooter who stood nearby. And he was right. It was a hen. How I trembled with fear, thinking that the doctor would be furious with me. But he only said "I'm sorry."

There were more pheasants hit. The beaters collected them with the help of boys and put them in the cart, which was very similar to those used in the French Revolution. It bore this inscription: Lord S., M.C.

"For what did Lord S. get his M.C.?" I asked. Dr. Boswell took his pipe out of his mouth: "He was the first Englishman to shoot a German in the last war. He was leading the Guards when suddenly they saw the German cavalry advancing towards them. Lord S. commanded his soldiers to hide and not to shoot until he gave them the word. Then as the Germans advanced he shot and immediately hit the German officer. His soldiers finished the job and they brought home ten German horses." Having finished this story, which reminded me of the good old times of gentlemanly warfare, he replaced his pipe and puffed away contentedly. "Is Lord S. wealthy?" I asked. "I wouldn't say so, he has only 8,000 acres," Dr. Boswell answered.

Once again we formed a line; once again we began to shoot. The old doctor shot at everything that flew up. By good luck they were all cocks. But he did not always hit. The rain increased. My boots were full of water and mud. I was hungry. At the end it was said we were going to a farm.

What a farm! It was just a barn. When we entered, their lordships, commodores and colonels tried to find seats on some dirty sacks and began to take food from their haversacks. Then, unlike tramps, they began to talk politics, but as usual in a very light-hearted manner. They joked as if there was nothing serious in the world. "I am not interested in politics," I whispered to Dr. Boswell. "Will you introduce me to that lady sitting on that upturned barrel?" "I will not," said the doctor. "This is a shooting party, not a petting party."

We finished our meal and went out into the pouring rain to shoot once again. Suddenly we heard a horrible explosion. Bombs? Dr. Boswell swore. At that moment there appeared in the sky two monsters, grey and frightening. What could they possibly be? Only Junkers 87. "Fetch them down," shouted the doctor. And before you could say Jack Robinson, bang, bang, went two shots from his gun. "Good Lord, they are Wellingtons," I cried as if I wanted to tell him they were hens and not cocks. "I'm sorry," replied the brave doctor. "But aren't I a plucky devil – I wasn't afraid even though there were two of them."

Darkness was beginning to fall as we returned from the English shooting party. "Wasn't I right when I told you that English shooting parties were quite different from yours?" asked Dr. Boswell. "Absolutely right," I answered with resignation.

JAN KOSMA

A WAY TO WAKEN SILENTLY
(1977)

Sir, Sixty years ago while serving in the then North-West Mounted Police on the Ukon Trail I met an old prospector who, in his youth, had been an Indian fighter in the States. I asked him how a change of sentries could be made silently in the night without giving the position away. The tip he gave me was this. Ease and feel – that is pinch – the lobe of the ear several times, and even the heaviest sleeper seems to come awake without panic. He maintained that a nerve in the lobe of the ear seems to "telegraph" the message to the brain. I found it worked.

T. V. FLEMING

*Sir, The method described by Captain Fleming of waking,
without startling, a sleeping man by pinching the lobe of his ear
differs slightly from that taught me by my father. His method, which
he learnt in the South African War, was to press lightly with the
thumb or knuckle the hollow behind the lobe of the sleeper's ear.*

*I seem to remember also that Pieter Pienaar, the old Boer hunter
who figures in* Greenmantle *and some of John Buchan's other novels,
is said to use this method when danger threatened.*

*As Captain Fleming says, it works like a charm and, instead of
starting up with a snort, an oath and a clatter, the sleeper merely
opens up the eyes, at the same time becoming fully awake and alert.*

*I taught my men the trick in the last war. Once a sentry thought
he heard a Jerry patrol cutting the wire in front of our position. By
using the "patent method" the rest of the platoon was awakened and
moved to the stand-to position without a sound.*

*As it happened, the noise which the sentry took for the snick of
wire-cutters was caused by nothing more formidable than a ram
caught by its horns in the triple dannert. Needless to say he provided
a welcome addition to our rations for the next few days.*

C. MACKENZIE SMITH

A GIRL IS OUT OF PLACE IN A STABLEYARD
(1938)

To me a girl is out of place in a stableyard, for it is a rough
place, where beer and bad language flow. Picking up
droppings and dressing horses are not jobs for the fair sex. As
I have remarked, they are not found much with hunters,
which is a good thing, for doing a hunter and its tack after a
dirty day is hard work, needing the expenditure of much
energy; that is, if it is to be properly done. Personally, I do
not think girls are physically suited to hard stable work, and I
should not care to have any girl I cared for or respected
round about when the cussin' and blindin' start.

These girls frequently work with horses not of necessity,
but just because they like it and it gives them something to

do. They usually perform their duties for a small wage, and sometimes for nothing. Erstwhile, this was poaching on an able-bodied man's job, and causing unemployment where it ought not to be; but now, of course, with the industrial revival perhaps it is different, though even girl grooms do not seem so plentiful as heretofore.

Women are generally more exacting to work for than men, and usually more money-minded. They want the maximum value for the wage they pay, which, more often than not, is less than a man pays, and some complain that they are not so generous with their tips. They can be very meticulous and fault-finding. Nevertheless, it is rather enchanting after a hard day's work on hunters, if the pretty lady comes out to the stables to see and inquire how the hunters are; and even if she does fault-find us, we can bear it, for her presence is a tonic for our sore eyes and tired bodies, and brings a ray of sunshine into our drab lives. But, of course, if she does not fault-find us, and is gracious instead, from thenceforth we become her devoted slave. Believe me, a kind word can work wonders, and a kind word from without a pretty face can perform miracles.

One sometimes wonders, without wishing to be ungallant, whether the term pretty lady is applicable to the present-day sex complex visions one bumps into, with their plucked eyebrows, false lashes, lifted faces, painted cheeks, vermilion-gashed mouths, and finger nails akin to the talons of the eagle which has been clawing at its prey. For all beauty comes from God and nature, by which it is adorned and decked. Fresh air, the wind, the rain, and the sunshine bring roses to the cheeks and a lustre to the eyes, which artificial beauty culture can never do, and that all too rare phenomenon the English sunshine brings glints and tints from without the glory of my lady's tresses, which will gladden the eye of the simple countryman who gazes thereon.

To you, mesdames, perhaps an old sweat may be permitted to give a word of advice, which may at times save both you and your grooms discomfiture. Never approach a stable unawares: always give warning of some sort of your pending arrival, such as an audible cough at a distance. This is not to warn us to put our cigarettes away in case we should be smoking, but in order that your finer and more sensitive feelings may not be hurt by the continual cussin' and blindin' that will probably be going on within. Grooms, I suppose, should not curse and swear; nevertheless, they nearly all do – a prerogative, I imagine, handed down to them through the ages, which, all the same, they do not care about blasting upon the dainty ears of a fair lady.

R. M. S. BARTON

MY FIRST AMERICAN FOOTBALL GAME
(1920)

Although I have visited American universities, and have, as I supposed, witnessed many typical scenes both before and since the war, I was told that if I had not seen an American college football game my experiences were pitiably incomplete. I was informed that I was not fitted to go back to England possessed of a clear-cut notion of American enthusiasm until I had been to a football game.

I was conducted to a game between the universities of Illinois and Iowa, on the home ground of the former, situated in the heart of the richest corn-belt in the world. The geographical situation of this university at Champaign was born in upon me by the fact that we had to drive fifty miles through corn. Corn to starboard, corn to port, the vast tract only relieved by the three townships of Le Roy, Farmer City and Mahomed, all perfectly dry islands in this sea of corn. There had been no rain for months, so the earth was dry, the corn was dry, the roads were dry, and my throat got drier and drier. I revelled in it. I pulled out my packet of Camel cigarettes and gazed at it long and admiringly – at the corn coloured camel, at the corn coloured pyramid, and at the corn coloured sand depicted on the wrapper, and each successive cigarette was working me up for the climax, my arrival at Champaign.

The roads were blocked by cars filled to overflowing with students, bright-eyed and brilliant-cheeked girls being conspicuously in evidence. There is co-education at Champaign, and there are some 10,000 students. Just think of Lady Margaret Hall and Somerville and Nuneham and Girton all let loose in fast motor cars driven by undergraduates down the streets of Oxford and Cambridge.

The ground was already packed by the time we came to take our seats. There was a brass band, composed of about sixty members of the student body, complete with all Sousa's special instruments, on the touch-line. Rather than the band being subservient to the sport, as is usually the case at big football games in England, everyone and everything hung on the conductor's baton. This man ruled the 8,000 odd people present with his strip of cane as though he were at a traffic control post on 5th Avenue. One moment he would be dancing on one foot, the next he would be standing at attention, his baton "at the carry" and his other hand uplifted as only George Robey in archidiaconal mood knows how.

The two teams filed onto the ground. Everyone rose: the pontiff himself, accompanied by all his satellites and acolytes, could not have commanded more respect. The band struck up the university song, and the assembled host gave tongue. Cinematograph operators and photographers dashed madly about, knocking each other's hats off in their endeavours to secure the best position. Others were rushing crates of water-bottles across the ground, whilst the numerous officials took up the attitude so typical of a mayor and corporation prepared to welcome an arctic explorer or the creator of a new state.

Finally, after considerable organised cheering on both sides, the game commenced. The ball, of similar shape to our Rugby ball, was kicked off from the centre of the ground in the direction of the goal posts, similar in design to our Rugby goal posts. There the immediate similarity in the two games began and ended.

There are only eleven players on each side; instead of there being only "half time," there is "quarter time," when the sides change over. The "scrum" does not form in a three-two-three phalanx, but is spread out in line. The centre man holds the ball, and after having shouted directions to his own side in a number code, which may cause them to change positions in the line, and in consequence their tactics also, he passes it back between his legs to a "three quarter" back, who runs with the ball until he is brought to earth, generally with a resounding thud. If, after the knotted skein of legs and arms has been disentangled by the umpire, the referee decides that 10 yards has been gained (the ground is marked out from the goal to goal in parallel white chalk lines 10 yards apart), the side having gained the ground maintains hold of the ball for the next play. If a "down", as it is called, has been achieved, the fans of the successful side will have been called upon by their cheer leaders to give forth a yell such as the following:

Os kee wow wow!
Skin nee wow wow!
Illinois! Illinois!
Yaaae!

The band then takes up the matter with a tune similar to that evolved after a comedian has just concluded a successful turn. It may be possible for the side which has made a "down", provided that certain tenets of the rules have been complied with, to initiate a few minutes rest, whereupon the spectators are reintroduced to the crates of water bottles, which are rushed to the ground, and the players, having divested themselves of their leather head pieces, indulge in a mouth-rinsing and squirting competition.

The cheer leaders will then call upon their followers for another yell, the efficacy of which appears greatly to depend on whether the antics of the leaders are satisfactory or not. If they display sufficient pep – that is to say, if they contrive to turn themselves almost inside out in the process, the response will be correspondingly vociferous. The spectators are then allowed for a brief spell to concentrate on watching the game. But fortune is fickle, and one side or the other may suddenly do something good. It is up to the fans then to do their bit again. A "try" (6 points) may have been scored and the goal kick converted (another point) and then pandemonium! its culminating point being the double "B" yell as follows:

Double "B" Yell
Brrrrrrrrrrrrrrrr BOOM!
Brrrrrrrrrrrrrrrr BOOM!
Yaaaaaaa
ILLINOIS (pause with leader) ILLINOIS
Brrrrrrrrrrrrrrrr BOOM!
Illinois rah, rah; Illinois rah, rah;
Illinois rah, rah, rah, rah, rah, rah.
ILLINOIS (pause with leader) ILLINOIS
(Start slowly)
ILLI yea rah yeah rah
NOIS yea rah yea rah;
ILLI yea rah yea rah,
NOIS yea rah yea rah,
ILLINOIS
Yea rah yea rah
ILLINOIS! YEA!
Go, ILLINI, Go!
Go, ILLINI, Go!
Oskee wow wow! Illinois!
GO!

The sun was particularly hot for October. I was beginning to perspire after that. My throat was feeling parched. Up to the present, the nearest I had got to any refreshment was in watching other people swill out their mouths with water. I was to dance into the early hours at the "φ ψ" fraternity after the game, and knowing full well that the spectators display 50 per cent of the energy expended during the course of a game, how was it to be done? That last "Illinois Go!" was still resounding in my ears. Personally, I felt that I would go anywhere, even to the place where the coal situation is always in hand, to have a little quiet. But I wouldn't have missed it for the world.

OUR CORRESPONDENT IN THE UNITED STATES

SHOOTING AND SMOKING
(1940)

Smoking is held by some people to be just a bad habit. Well, it may be; but, at any rate, it is a pleasant one, just as drinking is, I suppose, to the drunkard. There is not the slightest doubt that smoking by the individual who inhales a lot does his wind no good. To prove this, you have only to smoke a pipe whilst climbing up a steep slope and then notice how much more you puff and blow; for even by the man who does not inhale consciously a certain amount of smoke is absorbed into the lungs. But I inhale everything, pipe, cigar and cigarette – I should find no pleasure in smoking if I did not – and, though I may not have done my wind any good, I consider that it will last as long as I shall.

There is only one form of smoking which concerns the sportsman, whether he be shooter or fisherman, that is, the pipe, the only one that readily lends itself to the outdoor life. No one in his senses would dream of taking his choice Havana out in rain or damp; it is meant to be hot, but this one was not, and I smoked it for years, till, like the kitchenmaid's cup, it literally "fell to pieces in me 'and."

Think of that moment, non-smokers, when, having achieved that stiff climb through knee-high heather to the highest line of butts, knowing that you have a wait of at least twenty minutes before anything to shoot at can come along; you sit down on a patch of heather just outside your butt, pull your beautifully coloured briar out of your pocket, fill it with the mixture of your choice, light it and draw the resultant smoke deep into your lungs. Has anything ever tasted better? You know of better things? You're telling me! You sit in a dream, savouring the aroma of your baccy, at peace with the whole world, the smell of the heather mingling with the fragrant smoke. Truly a moment to be lived for!

Or another picture, outside a covert in December. The beaters are just starting at the other end of the wood, full three-quarters of a mile away; the afternoon is getting on, and already there is a slight mist coming down, and your baccy smoke seems to envelop you in a fragrant fog of pleasure. Apart from all these considerations, do not forget that the pipe gives one the best excuse for a missed shot. How often has one heard someone exclaim, on missing a sitter: "My pipe was in the wrong side of my mouth and hit my gun."

Let me end by quoting what John Addington Symonds said: "I am a devotee of the pipe, I have always found it conducive to good fellowship and sober thinking."

LOWLANDER

THE OPPOSITION
(1970)

People who believe that fishing is a peaceful, blameless, patient and contemplative sport (it has been called all four) will believe anything. On the contrary, it produces more passionate feelings than any other. This is due to the behaviour of other anglers rather than to that of the fish.

Single-bank salmon beats are among the most inflammatory factors, and the characters who loom all too large across the river are not known as the Opposition merely because of their situation. One-upmanship over them can become as important as catching fish. There are tales of total warfare breaking out, of ghillies brawling, and anglers throwing baits at one another, but I hope these stories are apocryphal.

All Oppositions, whatever the river or conditions, seem to have some things in common. One of these is an illusion that all the fish are lying under the other bank. Of course, one knows well that the best taking places are their side of the current; why else would one be treading water whilst throwing a perilously long line?

When the other fisherman is reasonably close, the proper drill is to wave him through with a gracious gesture (good manners always pay), thereafter remaining in the river, or close at hand. Perhaps he may become unsettled by one's unblinking stare. Like being allowed through at golf, it can be unnerving and result in a mistimed cast which produces a bird's nest, a tuft of the bank, or a fly caught on the top of the rod. Such moments make any Opposition temporarily tolerable.

I believe firmly in telepathy. Why else does one always find the Opposition making a move towards the same pool as oneself? It is undignified and difficult to run in waders in full view of the other side. When the path is fringed with bushes one can break into a trot, but this plays havoc with the breakfast kipper.

People fishing the fly opposite may have annoying habits, but bait slingers arouse the strongest emotions. Unless there is a specific agreement to the contrary, they have a perfect right to spin whatever the height of the water. There is, however, something infuriating about having a piece of shining metal thrown at one.

Looks and mannerisms are magnified across a river. As one smiles, primly if not inwardly, at the antics of a stout man skipping happily from rock to rock, it is as well to remember one is also being viewed through an equally distorted lens. Perhaps there is something to be said for wearing waders in this age when everyday clothes leave nothing to the imagination.

Once, at a dinner party, I was talking fishing to my next-door neighbour when we were interrupted by a bellow from the man sitting opposite who had overheard our conversation: "So you are the pretty poppet!" As far as I knew I had never met him, so I looked startled. So did his wife, and my husband. It transpired he had fished opposite me the previous year, and this was the nickname I had been given. There can be worse, especially from the Opposition.

Once, too, when fishing with a girl friend, we had a colonel fishing opposite us. We knew nothing about each other apart from some inaccurate ghillie gossip. We came across him one Sunday scanning our hotel register in a determined effort to find names to fit the bodies inside the waders. We all repaired to the bar and became friends.

One evening, at dusk, I hooked a fish in an awkward place with a hole between me and the bank. My first reaction was a yelp of horror, whereupon there was a shout from the opposite bank with an offer to swim to my aid. I could see the colonel preparing to do just this, so I pulled myself together, got out, and landed my grilse double quick.

I was spurred on by the thought of what village gossip would have been made of the incident should anyone have seen the colonel, in his underpants, and me together at 11 o'clock at night. Had the fish been bigger, the offer might have been accepted; which goes to show that the Opposition may even have its uses.

GEORGINA ROSE

TO THE AID OF THE PARTY
(1965)

Most people agree that Members of Parliament fall into two distinct categories. One is composed of immaculate archangels and the other of owners of horns and tails. Anyhow, there they are, and if they would stay at Westminster and let us get on with our jobs how happy we would be!

But they will ring up the barker outside their constituency booth, whose job it is to drum up custom, and ask him what the evening's takings look like. "Good Heavens," they say, "Is that all? For the love of Pete, have a bazaar to separate the faithful from their loose change," and that is how the trouble starts.

We villagers first learn that we have been grouped with three other politically-inert hamlets and are expected to ante-up things for a stall representing a country chemist's shop. Since notices produce nothing, one goes round beating on doors and asking for gifts, and after an hour one has become wary.

To say that any gift will be acceptable is to risk being offered a bottomless dustbin and a wheel-less pram. A refusal will give great offence and, if one accepts them, those manning the pseudo-country chemist's shop will wave them away. So a long morning's work with the begging-bowl leaves one the temporary owner of a pot of jam, 10 lb. of windfalls and a huge feather mattress to which, one is informed, many duck have contributed.

My valuation of the last of these gifts was lower than the smallest coin of the realm, but, surprisingly, the female element welcomed it. "It will make a dozen small cushions," they cried. "They will sell like hot cakes; all we need is some pretty material," and prattle unbridled broke out. I would be told when and where to produce it and, in the meanwhile, I would be good enough to store it in a warm, dry place. In pursuance of this order, I rammed it into the garage cupboard alongside the tennis posts, sprinkled it with rat-poison and dismissed it from my mind.

Two months later I received fresh orders. Of course the mattress was clean, but it would be a very good selling point if they could say that all feathers had been recently disinfected. They had rung up the Ministry of Health and given them my name and an expert would come soon. He arrived an hour later, driving a sports car in a manner that raised a bow-wave of gravel.

"I could find no record of a recent death," he said, "so I came straight out. Was it plague, typhoid or what?" He was a friendly soul and he grinned when he heard the truth.

"Ah, well!" he said tolerantly, "few people know the difference between disinfecting and disinfesting. Your mattress and its owners want psychological and not clinical treatment. Put it in a closed cellar, burn this candle and the thing will smell in a most hygienic way." He gave me a firework marked "Bad for greenfly" and rocketed off.

The mattress is vast. We fought it into the house, chucked it down the stairs and with much effort got it into the old tunnel where we force flowers. Then we lit the chemical candle and slammed the door. It is going to take a winch to get the thing up again, but I would rather do that than be one of those who will slit it up and shove the resulting snowstorm into cretonne sandbags.

There is no getting away from the fact that inadvertently, both MPs and duck can be great nuisances. Unfortunately, in this country one is allowed to shoot only the duck.

C. C. L. BROWNE

WILY WOODCOCK
(1942)

Must you always get up
From the green holly tree
At ridiculous moments
When no one is free?
Do you have to depart
With soft clattering rise
When the gun isn't cocked
And the sun's in my eyes?
Is it fair to escape
With a dip and a sway
While I trip in the brambles
That litter my way?
Will you never pick out
Some more suitable place
Where we could come to terms
In a clear open space?

HULDINE V. BEAMISH

November

WOMEN POACHERS
(1867)

The Ruthin police have made a curious capture. Sergt. Evans and two constables, having reason to suspect the home-coming of a gang of well known poachers, placed themselves on the highway near the town, and when the men came along, searched them without result. As it was obvious from the state of their clothes that they had been poaching, the officers again concealed themselves, and presently saw three women crossing the fields to a place where they remained some time. When they were returning the officers insisted on searching them. Their intelligence was amply rewarded, for the women had slung twenty-seven rabbits on three strings and tied them beneath their dresses. In this way they were also carrying off two long lengths of rabbit netting. They at the outset protested that the protuberances were ordinary "dress improvers" but the officers were obdurate, and at length the twenty-seven rabbits were produced. The women will be brought before the county magistrates on the charge of being in the illegal possession of game.

ANON.

175

ONE MAN AND HIS DOG
(1970)

He was an old man. His face could be likened not so much to a wrinkled apple as to smoked oak. His clothes were so neutral as to be nondescript, yet he was spry, and there was still a spring in his stride. He was as lean as the old cocker bitch by his side was plump; clearly even if he had gone without at times – and he probably had – she had not.

The old man was a real dog man, all his life he had had dogs, big ones, small ones, pedigree and mongrel, they had all come alike to him, but now, in his autumn years, he had returned to his old love, the cocker. He and his dogs had lived all their life in the country; he was part of it. He could lean against a tree and disappear. His dogs were always trained to fade away at the same time, and though the old cocker bitch had proved more difficult to train, she still managed to make herself scarce when it was needed.

The old man would have called himself a sportsman had anyone ever bothered to ask him what his occupation was, though he was worried as little by officialdom as he worried it. You would call him a poacher, though not to his face. The only ones who had got away with that over the years with impunity had been the chairmen of various magistrates' courts before which he had appeared on the rare occasions when he had been caught in compromising situations and had temporarily run out of either charm or excuses.

He was an incurable rogue, and had been all his life. He had never worked, as you or I work. His dwelling in the village, which had been permanent to him for the past 60 years, was by any other criterion, very temporary. It appeared to be constructed in the main from corrugated iron sheets and ancient meal sacks.

He had never married, feeling perhaps that he could not ask anyone other than his dog to share his casual existence in his somewhat primitive habitation. In his pride he always denied this, and when questioned over his daily pint, claimed that he had never met anyone good enough.

Even so, his simple dwelling was spotless inside and as warm and comfortable as anyone could wish. True, piped water and electricity were luxuries that he ignored, and on the rare occasions when, seen in the village in this time-reversed life, sleeping during the day, and working – as he called it – at night, he was usually carrying a paraffin tin. When his wood fire did not suffice, he cooked on an ancient oilstove, and always smelt faintly of an intriguing mixture of wood smoke, oil and tobacco.

On this particular evening he had already had his pint before his evening rounds. They were so accustomed to his habits in The George that as soon as he walked in, the landlord would draw his pint of brown ale and bring out Bess's dish. It was probably this constant imbibing of small quantities of the rich brew that had kept her as rotund as she was. It certainly helped her to keep her rich glow on her unusual dark liver colour – possibly she had a touch of Sussex spaniel in her background.

All his cronies were in the bar, and greeted him with the usual simple country jibes about the huge trout that used to live under the footbridge before he came to the village, and the strange shortage of rabbits this year. He ignored them as he always did. His business was his business, and no-one else's.

The pint finished, and both having well licked their whiskers, they disappeared down the lane in the gathering dusk, and both his fustian and her dark coat became just part of the background. He had always had dark-coloured dogs, red for preference, and the darker the better. He knew that they blended with the landscape in the dark areas he frequented; blending was his business.

Half a mile through the wood, every inch of which they both knew as well as they knew the inside of their hut, they arrived at a gate leading to the paddock at the back of a big house. The squire was in London: the old man had seen him leave on the early morning train from the shelter of one of his own coverts. He was the modern version of "Squire," a business man in town, who had bought the estate for the fishing and shooting that it offered. He knew the old man by sight only and had never spoken to him, though he guessed that they both had their sport in the same woods and rivers, but he left that sort of thing to his gamekeeper.

Bess was getting old and, after the initial rush of blood to the head that the familiar woods always produced, she had settled down to her now habitual plod. The old man knew that neither of them would last for ever, but had a shrewd idea that he would outlast her by some years. Hence this excursion.

The gamekeeper was in public the old man's sworn enemy, in private one of his closest friends. They had many years ago come to a perfect understanding, so long as the old man stuck to rabbits and the occasional hare, and so long as he left the birds and salmon alone, snaring pike as only he knew how, the gamekeeper would turn a blind eye to his activities. They never even acknowledged one another in the street, but lowered the level of many a bottle of the squire's whisky in his kitchen, the gamekeeper having what is called an understanding with the housekeeper.

The gamekeeper had pulled a fast one with the squire's favourite bitch. The squire wanted her mated with a winning dog in the area, being one for a smart-looking dog at all costs. The gamekeeper had other views, wanting to breed only the best workers. Whilst paying deference to the squire's wishes, he had taken her to what he called the "posh" dog when he knew very well she would not mate, and had mated her, when he knew she was right, to a son of Bess's in the next village.

She had whelped that morning, but unfortunately one of the pups was Bess's colour, and even the squire would smell a rat if he saw it, so the gamekeeper had sent word down to the old man to collect it quickly; this is where he was going when we first saw him. He was the complete expert at hand-rearing; Bess would nurse anything from a kitten to a squirrel, and tonight, on the rabbit-skin rug in front of the warm fire in the old hut behind the bakery, there would be another mouth to feed.

Harry Glover

YELLOW PERIL – THE INGRATITUDE OF A FOX
(1938)

I christened him Yellow Peril partly because of his curious colour – in sunlight he looked almost as golden as a Jaffa orange – and partly because he possessed to an amazing degree the cunning, the courage and the ferocious cruelty which have always distinguished the descendants of the Samurai.

I had known him from cubhood, when, as a tiny pink-eared bundle of yellow wool, he used to play with his brothers and sisters at the mouth of the big earth in Oldham Wood, where he was born. All the other members of his family were gone – some killed, others migrated to different parts of the country. He alone remained to be a plague and a menace to all the farmsteads around.

His crowning achievement was to leap over the orchard wall in broad daylight and, seizing Jemima, my fattest Aylesbury, by the neck, essay to leap back with her. In this foul deed he was foiled by the garden boy who, being in the orchard, hurled a large divot of earth at his head, thereby causing him to drop his prey. The noise that ensued – Jemima quacking, hens clucking, boy yelling and dogs barking –

brought me out of the house in time to see a small yellow object float down off the wall as lightly as an autumn leaf and disappear across the neighbouring fields.

"This," I said to myself, "becomes intolerable!" and I forthwith sat down and wrote a letter to Lord Essendon, our MFH, informing him of the depredations of the Yellow Peril, and begging him to come and draw the neighbouring covert as soon as possible.

Nevertheless, when, a fortnight later, hounds met in the village and moved off towards Oldham Wood, I had an utterly ridiculous sensation of having betrayed an old friend. And when, five minutes after they entered the covert, I espied a well-known yellow figure emerge from the wood and go swiftly skimming across the grass field beyond, I would, if I could, have prevented Jack, the second whip, from uttering that yell of "Garn away!" which proclaimed that our quarry was afoot. The hounds came pouring out of the covert like a beautiful mottled wave, with that screaming ecstasy which to those who love hunting is the most soul-stirring music in the whole world.

But to-day, as I galloped out of the covert in pursuit of hounds, I felt no thrill of pleasure in the chase. I knew how cunning the yellow fox was, and I prayed that he might shake off the pursuit of his enemies – yes, even if it meant the death of every duck I possessed. I realised to the full how preposterously inconsistent I was. As we swung along in all the speed and fury of full-cry I told myself foxes were beasts of prey, to hunt or to be hunted. Far better for him, I told myself, to die like this than to be mutilated in a trap or, blinded by a gun, die by inches as I had seen one unfortunate fox lately.

As a matter of fact, I do not believe the Peril took our pursuit of him very seriously. After leading us a circular tour over the worst line he could have found, he elected to hark back whence he had come and went to ground in a big rabbit bury only a mile from Oldham. The Master sent for the terriers, and turned to me with a glint in his eye. "Now your ducks will be avenged!" he said grimly.

He reckoned, however, without the boldness and quickness of this prince of foxes. They dug, and they dug, and they dug, while the terriers shrieked defiance down in the bowels of the earth, and the rabbit bury showed signs of stretching nearly to Australia.

Suddenly, like a torpedo from a gunboat or a cork from a champagne bottle, the Yellow Peril burst from the hole, cannoned against the master (neatly throwing him on his back), ricochetted between the legs of the first whip, slid like a shadow through the snapping jaws of eighteen couple of hounds, and disappeared from sight before we could even realise what had happened.

But he had been in the bury for nearly 20 minutes and had grown stiff. Furthermore, scent had greatly improved, and the hounds, mad for blood, were after him like a pack of wolves. I realised that he had little hope of escape, and not caring to see him killed, I turned my horse for home. As so often happens on these occasions the hunt seemed to pursue me, and as I rode up the drive to my house I heard hounds in full cry only a few fields away. I had given my horse to the groom and was crossing the stable-yard when a draggled yellow object came slowly crawling round the corner and vanished like a wraith into the open door of the wood-shed.

Hurriedly I slammed and bolted the door and ran down the drive, just as the Master and the pack with half the field behind them, swept into it from the road.

"Your fox," I gasped, purple in the face, "the gardener headed him – he's gone left through the village – chased by my dogs!" Lord Essendon thanked me (oh, shame! oh, shame!) and withdrew with his hounds and much doubling of his horn in the direction I had indicated; and I saw them no more.

Half an hour later when all was quiet I returned to the wood-shed, unlocked the door and flung it wide. "Come out, you rascal!" I cried; "and never expect me to do this again!"

From the wood-shed came no sound or movement, but in the shadowed darkness at the far end I perceived two baleful yellow eyes glaring at me with unquenchable hatred and distrust. I retired leaving the door open. The next morning I found that the Yellow Peril had gone; but alas! not alone, for he had taken Jemima with him.

Eva Dunbar

NOT QUITE LIKE THE BLAZERS
(1969)

Most Irish activities consist as much of talk as of action. Certainly this applies to the Monaghan Hunt who could probably out-talk a combined team of bores from the Meath, the Kildare or the Galway Blazers. That is not to say that their exploits would compare with the excitement of these eminent Irish packs, for on the several occasions I have been out with "The Hunt," nothing has happened. Yet this in no way reduces the theories on what is happening, might have happened, or happened last time.

It is the early stages of the hunt which are most difficult – finding the participants, or, if they fail to turn up, releasing their dogs from a farmyard shed and risking attack from dogs, sows and fighting cocks.

Mostly they arrive after Mass on Sundays in their dark Sunday best, some of them after a five-mile walk from the Cathedral. Others come on bicycles which they continue to use as horse substitutes throughout the day. Though no members of the Hunt can ride a horse, they are far from immobile.

Attendance suffers heavily from rival activities. Early in the season there is the potato digging and bringing in the corn stocks. A Sunday football match in Ballybay can paralyse the Monaghan and once, after a wedding reception in Castleblayney, the huntsman, Paddy McMahon, was suggested by someone to be stocious drunk. Only his hounds were disturbed. However, he emerged and took command of events.

How the Monaghan collect at the beginning of the day is a mystery as great as the migration of lemmings. Nothing is pre-arranged and they hunt different land each Sunday. It hardly matters, though, for the hunt is never cohesive but consists of a number of factions fragmenting and regathering to pool their information throughout the day.

Monaghan, or Muineachan in Irish, means "town of little hills" and the surrounding country is ideal for the huntsman who does not ride and will not run. On the day of the hunt a cluster of dark figures can be seen silhouetted on each hill against the skyline. Although they are restricted to the roads, it is the cyclists who become the best travelled and best informed as they go like battle messengers from one hill to the next, gleaning the best from each school of thought, and from farms as the hunt passes by.

The purpose of the hunt is not clearly defined, but it is generally agreed that if the hounds disappear in a straight line over the horizon in the direction of Carrickmacross and are not seen again, then it is a fox they are after. Ideally they describe a large circle round a dozen or more fields, preferably round the bottom of the hill on which one is standing. This means the hounds, or harriers as they should be but are rarely called, have found a good hare.

If they appear to be locked in the small field by briars and hawthorn hedges, it is a young hare which does not know the ground. It has probably never been out of that field and it needs to be trained. "Let the dog see the hare," said one man, raising his foot. It revealed an exhausted grey animal with ears back as it cowered in the rushes. Though he took good care to frustrate the hounds and see that they did not catch it as it made off, it was clearly a rare event in the pack's life for them to see the hare, and clearer still that they needed more training than it did.

In October when the hunt starts, the sole purpose seems to be to get the hounds and, more important, the hare – for they are known individually – fit. The only hares I saw at close range were three which ran down the road past our feet. The ensuing scramble to open and shut gates, put hounds off the scent and give the hare a chance, was the most violent activity seen.

The movement of the hounds in straight lines, or large or small circles is clearly understood. It is when they go in separate directions that speculation begins, for each man believes implicitly in his own hounds. Whatever happens, no-one blames the hounds, for that would destroy the unique harmony of the Hunt which, unlike most Irish gatherings, has neither money nor pride at stake.

JAMES HUGHES-ONSLOW

EL ZORRO
(1940)

During a fast hunt with the Royal Calpe Hounds last Friday, I heard a shot fired in front of hounds, and galloping round some bushes was confronted by an excited Spanish sportsman, holding in one hand a smoking gun and in the other his sombrero. He rushed up to me shouting: "A thousand pardons Señor, I missed the fox but he is only a short way ahead and your dogs may yet catch him."

AN OFFICIAL OF THE ROYAL CALPE HUNT

SPELLING PTARMIGAN AND WIGEON
(1940)

Sir, A recent Government order refers to the killing of "tarmagan"; this method of spelling is new to me and I should be interested to know if it is correct, since presumably the Government draughtsman would have good reason for employing it. The King's English Dictionary *does not give this form of spelling, but the more common one "ptarmigan" with the alternative "tarmigan" from the Gaelic "tarmachan." Have you any information on the subject?*

DUDLEY

Sir, I enclose the explanation of the spelling of Ptarmigan as given in two English dictionaries.

Shorter Oxford English Dictionary, *1933: Ptarmigan = Gael. Tarmachan. History and origin unknown. Spelling with pt arises from false analogy.*

Universal Dictionary of the English Language, *1934: Ptarmigan. Gael. tarmachan. The excrescent "P" appears in French, possibly due to Greek Pterón, wing, found frequently in zool.*

The French form of the word is the same as ours. There is no similar word in German – schneehuhn is used. I confess that I never saw the spelling tarmigan even in Scotland.

G. H. CLARKE

Sir, You will find in "A Treatise on the Law of Scotland as applied to the Game Laws, etc.," by John Hunter Tait, 1901:

"... or have in his possession or use any muirfowl or tarmagan" which later is described as "tarmargan or ptarmigan."

EDWARD PATON & SON

Sir, In The Acts of the Parliaments of Scotland, *1124–1707, the spelling of ptarmigan appears as follows: James VI (1599), Termiganis; James VI (1600) Termiganis; James VI (1621) Termigantis; James VII (1685) Tormichan.*

Sir Robert Sibbald in his Scotia Illustrata sive prodromus Historiæ Naturalis *(1684) spells it Ptarmigan and he is followed by most subsequent authors.*

HUGH S. GLADSTONE

Sir, Until the last ten years, I had always seen the spelling "widgeon." The Concise Oxford Dictionary *gives no other spelling.*

As to the derivation, this authority states, "cf. Pigeon and French vigeon, vinceon, which however are not recorded as Eng. widgeon. This suggests that "vigeon" is taken from English: "vigeon" is not given in the Concise Oxford French Dictionary *(1934).*

C. J. SAUNDERS

Sir, I was much interested in your two letters on spelling "ptarmigan" and "wigeon."

Ptarmigan is certainly derived from the Gaelic as "càrn," a heap of stones or cairn. Tarmachan,the Gaelic name, merely means "cairn-bird" and the name is apt.

The fact that widgeon is now spelled wigeon became known to me only lately when I was looking over the revised MS of my new book. I had used the spelling widgeon at least a score of times, and most probably will have to pay for my mistake.

DUGALD MACINTYRE

Sir, The dictionaries appear to favour the "d" while such authorities as Morris, Hudson, Jourdan and Thorburn, to mention a few, omit the "d." The Admiralty, scholars no doubt but possibly not ornithologists, evidently perused the dictionary before naming H.M.S. Widgeon a few years ago.

H. M. CLUTTERBUCK

ON THE 'PHONE
(1954)

Some years ago, in a work of fiction which can best be dismissed as fancied, I portrayed the noble but eccentric owner of a grouse moor using a field telephone in his butt to commune with his butler, or his stockbroker, or his lady love, during the duller earlier moments of a grouse drive. For this suggestion I was taken to task, very friendlily in a letter, by no less than the late Sir Hugh Gladstone, one of the best known, and certainly one of the most knowledgeable sportsmen of the last 50 years. I could not help feeling that Sir Hugh had strained at the gnat of my field telephone and swallowed the camel of my story as a whole. But now, as nature always seems to have anticipated art, a friend who once lived at Culford has sent me a cutting, found in his father's old game books, which was published in a transatlantic journal before the first war.

This is headed "Telephones and Pheasants," and begins: "Telephones connect all the shooting butts at Elveden Hall, near Bury St. Edmunds, Suffolk, England, where King George went recently for his customary shooting visit to the Earl of Iveagh. This 20,000 acre preserve, where the King has gone shooting every fall for 30 years, abounds in woodcock, partridge and pheasant, and the shoots are conducted in the most scientific manner.

"Every covert is connected up by a system of telephones to aid the birdseekers. When game is flushed by one gun, it is possible immediately to telephone a near-by shooter to be on his guard. Automobiles are used to convey the guns from drive to drive, for the different beats, and at noon motor cars hand hot lunches to that part of the wood where the sportsmen are assembled." It is a delightful picture, if one can imagine the "birdseeker" hurriedly dropping the receiver to come into action and wipe his neighbour's eye.

The march of science is so swift that at times it leaves us gasping behind. The radio-telephone, for example, is now an established adjunct at Badminton and other hunter trials. Poor Mrs. X stands, shivering and apprehensive, at the water jump and knows, as does the whole crowd, that her husband, or her daughter, has taken three refusals at the coffin, or fallen at the quarry, when she is two long miles away from any chance of comforting them or the horse. A "walkie-talkie" radio is also in use, I am told, on at least one famous shoot, whereby the host can commune with his keeper during the very progress of a partridge drive. No longer need he wait blindly behind a hedge or belt for half an hour, wondering what is happening to the beaters or the birds.

We are prone to dismiss such phenomena by saying "It will be all the same in a hundred years." But alas, it will not. Will the foxhunter of 1970 carry a pocket radio on his saddle instead of a sandwich case, so that he can telephone for his second horse or horse-box? Will there ever come a day when the field, clustered on the upwind side of a huge woodland, will learn, by radio, what the huntsman is doing half a mile away downwind? It might be very convenient. For homes have been broken up before now because the Master would detail his own wife or daughter to canter off and watch some unlikely corner of a covert, and there she would go on waiting, fuming and drenched and disconsolate, with the wind blowing so hard that she could not hope to hear his horn, when everyone moved on elsewhere.

Yet I for one hope that neither hunting nor shooting will get more and more "scientific," like the gadgets of total war. Perish the thought of a hunting horn that will blow itself, a shotgun or a rifle which makes its own "predictions" and adjustments of aim and fires a guided missile, a pair of hunting boots which need no jack, a warning light in your grouse butt just before the birds top the ridge, a mechanical ferret which will never lie up or need digging out, or perhaps a "self-closing" main earth, which will save all that frustration at the climax of a hunt into someone else's country. I trust that no "boffin" ever gets busy on the planning and design of field sports, as they have with aircraft carriers or golf.

J. K. STANFORD

ON BONFIRE NIGHT
(1964)

The village always celebrates Guy Fawkes's night with a thoroughness that stems from a determination to keep green the memory of the only man who ever thought up a really good joke about Parliament. We have fireworks round a gigantic bonfire and, in the background, tea and buns in the tin hut called the cricket pavilion.

This Babylonian orgy is run by the combined forces of the Mothers' Union, the Young Wives' Club and the Women's Institute, and very successful it is. There is no friction between these three branches because anybody who is a member of one is usually a member of the others, irrespective of whether they are schoolgirls, matrons or spinsters.

We all contribute our labour, and hard experience has taught me to which jobs one should sell a dummy. Last year it fell to us to make the guy and place him in position on the pyre. Beyond offering some old jungle-green drill and then locking my dressing-room door I was not concerned with the creation of the guy. My turn came when he and a 30 ft. ladder had to be humped to the site.

The makers of the fire had really surpassed themselves. The basis of it was 300 yds. of hedgerow which had been grubbed up, and the result must have been 40 ft. high, for my ladder did not reach to the top. It was a sagging, shifty edifice, and my progress up the ladder carrying a vast guy built around the pole was a dicey ascent. However, I eventually scaled the heights and, with a good deal of difficulty, rammed the pole into the tangled mass of branches.

As I reached the ground the guy bowed courteously to me and shed his bowler hat, so I reared the ladder up again and put things right. When I was half-way down he canted over to a flank the better to shake off a glove, so back I went and tied it on with baler twine. The vibration of my descent caused him to discard the other one and, my protests overruled, I was hounded up yet again to ensure that he was properly dressed.

I was just starting my third precarious descent when this jocund lay-figure of our creation sprang at me and swept me off my ladder. That I fell slowly and without injury was due to the braking effect of the brambles, holly and gorse that made up the fire, but I was a very scratched individual when I reached the ground, and it took nearly another hour to lash, prop and brace the brute in position.

He must have taken a dislike to my old bowler, because when the fire was lit he quickly nodded it off and a small boy snatched it up. I last saw it sailing away into the darkness on the nose of a rocket and as it never came down I presume that it is now in orbit somewhere.

Our guy this year is going to be a symbolic representation of Top of the Pops, a symphony of damp locks and dirty hands. Let him shake them off if he can!

C. C. L. BROWNE

LETTER FROM THE DANUBE
(1860)

Beware of frogs, ye settlers in strange lands ... In fact, this advice should be borne in mind anywhere before we fix upon a spot for our dwellings. "Mark Tapley" was, I imagine, the only man who considered a frog to be "rather a jolly animal," but to the minds of most people this creature is the embodiment of all that is cold, naked, wretched, and comfortless. In our natural kind-heartedness we pity his condition, and long to make him sit with his back to a good fire – but it would be the death of him: his ways are not our ways; he enjoys a day when we go splashing about, ankle-deep grumbling at the pelting rain, and feeling discontented with the world in general. This is the frog's delight, and he comes forth from his hiding place to revel in the wet. We are miserable on account of the weather; he is happy for the same reason. Thus it requires no great argument to prove that he delights in what you hate, that he is, in fact, really jolly when you are catching cold. Thus I say, "Beware of frogs." This is really no joke. If you are going to build a house, and you see a tempting spot, make a few enquiries about frogs, and whether they are plentiful. Search for them yourself, and if you find many, and satisfy yourself that they enjoy the locality, avoid it as you would a trap. You cannot live where the frog thrives, without ague and rheumatism.

For the last two months I have been living among frogs, as large as good-sized rats, and are literally in millions. This place, Medjidié, is situated on the Danube, abounding in shallow stagnant lakes and high reeds and bulrushes, forming a valley of some miles in length. This is one vast nursery for frogs, who are, in fact, the proprietors of the lakes. It is likewise one great nest where fevers, agues, and rheumatisms are bred for the curse of the human inhabitants of the neighbourhood. No-one would, therefore, covet a co-proprietorship with the frogs. They, like all people enjoying a monopoly, are assuming and bumptious, popping up their ugly heads in crowds as I go splashing after wild ducks, and croaking what doubtless means "all trespassers will be prosecuted" ....

It is a strange fact that, in spite of warnings, we frequently fall into nets which all see except ourselves. Thus our men were encamped at Varna, on the margin of the lake of Deona, at the same time the frogs were croaking death-warnings at their very feet. Why this folly? The fact is that without convenient vessels the carriage of water from a distance is tedious; men, therefore, pitch upon the nearest spot where it is obtainable, regardless of consequences. And thus the Tartars who arrived here in masses but a few weeks ago likewise commenced their encampments on the very verge of the swamps.

I prophesied misery to the Tartars in a recent report, but it has come upon them more quickly than I had anticipated. A virulent marsh-fever attacked them, and they died like flies in winter. Great numbers have been removed from this spot, and have passed up the Danube to be settled at Widdin. A large surface of ground, which only a few days ago was thickly studded with tents, is now entirely deserted, nothing remaining but a new and extensive burial ground, the result of only a few weeks' sojourn.

These people have a curious method of grave-digging. An ordinary grave of about five feet depth being excavated, they undermine at the bottom a sufficient space to receive a body; thus the grave appears to be empty, but the tenant is stowed away in the recess. All is then filled up, and a mound marks the spot as usual – the Tartar is at rest.

There appears to be a total disregard for human life, and no arrangements attempted for its preservation – no doctors, no medicine, but a blind faith in destiny, sour milk, and onions. What that destiny is may be readily imagined when malignant fever has no stronger drugs to combat with than the onions and curds. I had a conversation a short time ago with one of the old inhabitants of the country, a Turk, upon the subject, and it ran much as follows:

Question. – What do the public do in case of sickness, without medical aid?

Old Turk. – They eat onions and sour milk.

Question. – But in severe cases what remedies are usual?

Old Turk. – Sour milk and onions, as much as a person can eat.

Question. – But there must be cases when the eating of onions is impossible. What then is the course?

Old Turk. – Sour milk without the onions.

Question. – Surely there are special cases when medical assistance is required; for instance, your ladies must now and then be subject to the dangers of childbirth?

Old Turk. – We give them plenty of sour milk, and they get all right.

Question. – Is the mortality great in a percentage of the diseases?

Old Turk. – Not generally, unless during epidemics, such as fever or cholera.

Question. – What are your usual remedies for such diseases?

Old Turk. – Sour milk and onions.

Question. – Nothing but sour milk and onions?

Old Turk. – Sometimes cabbage soup, when we can procure the cabbages.

Question. – Why have you no resident medical man among you?

Old Turk. – We had one once, but more people died when he was with us than either before or since; therefore we are better without a doctor.

Question. – When your sour milk, &c., produces no good effect, do you seek no other assistance? What is your course?

Old Turk. – We are in the same position as the doctor when his drugs produce no effect: we trust in Allah. God is great!

... Next to the frogs in point of numbers, and inhabiting the same marshes in this neighbourhood, are the snipes, which at this season afford unlimited sport. The walking is, however, excessively bad, which somewhat destroys the pleasure of shooting. The marshes are overgrown with reeds, twelve or fourteen feet high, and of the texture of bamboo. These have been cut by the natives for thatch, leaving a kind of stubble some two feet long of sharp points, growing in a bog where a man sinks from a few inches to a foot deep at every step. The effects of the sharp points upon the shins may be conceived. My waterproof boots sprang a leak during the first half hour; they were pierced in several places, the water poured in at the sides and was unable to escape; accordingly, I was under the necessity of making a hold in the sole – in fact, scuttling them – and their glory has departed.

Fifteen couple of snipe in about two hours hardly repays a man for tearing his legs to pieces in such ground.

S. W. BAKER

SCOLOPAX
(1930)

The reason one misses this fowl is because
So often he's not where one thought that he was;
Or rather – to put it correctly – that he
Was not in the spot where one thought he would be,
You roll over rabbits again and again
As they trundle along on a permanent plain;
But a snipe may screw anywhere; how can you know?
To the right? To the left? Or above? Or below?
There's only one thing that is left you to do:
Choose a good spot of air which you hope he'll choose too.

SEMPER SPERANS

December

MAGPIES
(1920)

Sir, With reference to "Cheviot's" remarks about magpies in The
Field *December 11, the following rhyme, which I was taught when
young, may be of interest:*

> One for sorrow,
> Two for mirth,
> Three for a marriage,
> Four for a birth,
> Five for silver,
> Six for gold,
> Seven for love that never grows old.

*When living near Pembroke, where Magpies are very numerous,
I frequently saw as many as eight of them together, and remember on
one occasion my wife and I counted seventeen in a tree together, but I
think their presence was accounted for by a piggery in the next field.*

CAPTAIN G. C. PEARSON, RN

MAGPIES
(1920)

Magpies and their relation to the economics of game-preserving is a subject which has interested me ever since, as a boy, I first saw one of those big, domed nests, and was told by the keeper of his reason for watching at the corner of a particular ride. He was one of the old-fashioned sort, who strung up jays, stoats and weasels on lines among the trees, and who set traps which defiled the wood from fifty yards away. And he may have been right in what he believed about magpies; it may be that the magpie is what a writer in the Badminton Library says he is – a bird which should not be allowed to draw the breath of life on any estate where game is preserved, or words to that effect. All I can say is that he gave me no evidence. Not have I yet been able to obtain evidence which has seemed to me valuable as to the guilt of magpies in connection with partridges or their eggs. I do not say they are not guilty, but I have certainly talked to gamekeepers who say they do no harm; and as for personal experience during the last season, I had three magpies nests close to partridge nests, none of which was touched. One of these pests was in a larch, with a blackbird's nest in a bank within twenty yards, and the blackbird brought up three broods in the same nest.

But magpies have acquired a fresh interest for me in the last few days. On Sunday I saw what I believe to have been a number of magpies migrating. Of course, we have most of us seen magpies in small flocks; we all know the old proverb beginning "One for sorrow" but I think it does not count farther than four, and I imagine that magpies in really large flocks cannot be a common sight. Well, on Sunday I saw on the borders of Surrey and Sussex one of those large collections of magpies which some people believe are a legacy of the war, but which I am inclined to think have come together for a different reason. I came out from a ride in the wood to a field where you can generally see one or two magpies, and realised that there were more than one or two – enough, indeed, for more than one or two proverbs.

The birds kept flying from an elm in the corner of the field over to a wood on the other side, and I counted thirteen in the air at one time – a pretty sight, with their black-and-white plumage and their long tails quivering as they flew. Then I realised that from other trees other magpies were moving in the same general direction, travelling south-east. Altogether I counted twenty-one in the space of say five minutes and then the flight seemed to come to an end.

Now, did I hit on the only magpies in the district, all accidentally come together, or was this part of a larger flight moving from the north to winter quarters? Do magpies, like thrushes and robins, shift their ground in these islands at the change of the seasons, or do we get magpies in the winter from abroad, in the same way as we get wood-pigeons and stock-doves? Saturday and Sunday, it may be remembered, were days of high, cold winds from the north-west. Were these magpies migrating, and if so, to what winter quarters?

CHEVIOT

Sir, In your issue of December 11, "Cheviot," in an interesting article, raises the question as to whether magpies migrate in winter.

I do not profess to be much of a natural historian, but I beg leave to suggest that a bird which does not think it worth while to leave a place like Upper Deeside in mid-winter is not much of a migrant. I suppose that the Valley of the Dee from Ballater upwards is about as cold a district as any in the British Isles, excluding places like the top of Ben Nevis or Corrour or Fealair. Yet this district is full of magpies all the year round. Only to-day (Dec 13) I saw three of them in the course of a very short outing. It is almost impossible to go out any day here without seeing one or more of them at all times of the year. If the magpies which we see in winter are visitors, they must surely be Esquimaux birds; no other climate could rear birds so hardy as to consider Braemar warm at this time of year!

Cheviot mentions having seen twenty-one magpies at once in the Sussex border. Possibly it may be some natural custom for these birds to congregate at this time of year, because it so happens that once, about this time of year (to be exact, it was in late November 1917),

I saw an even greater number of magpies than Cheviot did, on the borders of Wiltshire and Dorsetshire. I was riding across Martin Down on the way from Salisbury to Wimborne St. Giles, with a companion, who, if he were not in India, would no doubt confirm this statement, when a flock of magpies crossed our path. He counted thirty-one, being quicker of sight than myself, and I counted twenty-nine. As far as I can remember, they seemed to be making from Pentridge Hill to Vernditch Chase, or from south to north. I think that it is more than possible that they had come from Vernditch Chase to start with, and were merely making back there again, and that the direction of their flight had no special significance. My observations since coming here would not lead me to suppose that they were migrating at any rate.

Cheviot also mentions a proverb connected with magpies. We count up to seven in Scotland as regards this proverb, not four. The lines run:

> One for sorrow,
> Two for mirth,
> Three for a wedding,
> Four for a birth,
> Five for Heaven,
> Six for Hell,
> Seven for the De'il his ainsel!

J. D. RAMSAY

AN EYE FOR AN EYE
(1942)

I protest that young Franklyn was no snob. He was just a normal young man with sporting tastes, and an agreeable manner. But when he was asked to stay at Strathhaggis he was elated. He did not broadcast it to all Brook Street, but all the same he was not angry when people found out about the duke's invitation.

Breakfast the first morning had set the pulse beat of ducal life. A sideboard of Homeric proportions was covered by an array of silver dishes warming to their little spirit lamps. To those who were brave enough to lift the lid of each, of all, they were found to contain every conceivable breakfast dish that ingenuity and His Grace's chef could devise. In the dish on the left of the line, reposing on a bit of toast, was a solitary snipe, round whose leg was tied a small label, "For His Grace."

Tommy Franklyn, nervously lifting the first lid, had happened on the snipe; he quickly replaced the lid with the furtive and ashamed stealth of one who wakes from slumber in church. But the dish held his fascinated gaze till His Grace made his morning entry, looking every inch (and alas! his inches were limited) the Chieftain.

Slowly he made his way along the whole ambrosial length of silver dishes. A slight but definite increase in the sound of replaced lids suggested that no favour was therein found, and at last he reached the dedicated snipe. Tommy's heart stood still. His Grace put back the lid and rang the bell. With silent precision a footman appeared. "I think I'll have a boiled egg."

After breakfast the party set out, and in riding from one line of butts to another, Tommy found himself next to Mary Malone. She put him through the usual catechism, found he knew enough of the right people, and opened out. "Wasn't it just too frightful for Jacko?" Tommy was sure it was, but why? Didn't he know? Hadn't he heard? Tommy didn't know and hadn't heard. And then it all came out.

Darling Jacko was the most careful shot in all the world. He had shot everywhere. For years and years. Well, yesterday, he went out at the pick-up, and the fool of a loader forgot to remind him his gun was still loaded. Well, he was talking to Cousin Mungo (His Grace's name) and his gun went off and killed Brech, Cousin Mungo's labrador, whom he simply adored. "What did he say!" asked Tommy. "He didn't say much. But I think his silences are worse, and everybody just looked at darling Jacko. And Jacko couldn't face it, so he just said he'd have to go today, and nobody tried to stop him, and now I shan't have any more fun...."

As Tommy, on his pony, rode to the top butt he pondered on the frightful fate of Jacko. What a fool. And yet, he thought, "There, but for the grace of God...." How awful if something like that were to happen to him. He who had quite made up his mind that Strathhaggis was to become an annual event. He might commit every sin in the social calendar, but his shooting must be safe.

The last line of butts before lunch was one of those maddening ones which have a long unending vista of slightly undulating heather over which the grouse packs come bobbing out of infinity, and all sense of distance and judgment is lost. A hundred yards in front of the butts was long patch of dead ground, sunk perhaps ten feet below the general level. It sank in a triumph of camouflage into the undulating purple beyond. His loader (could he be "the fool" who had left Jacko to his folly?) warned him that to avoid any possibility of accident the beaters held their flags above their heads as they emerged from the dip to prevent a chance last shot doing damage. No reference was made to His Grace's labrador, though both were thinking of it.

In a very few minutes, however, they were hard at it. The birds were streaming at them over the heather, and Tommy, thinking "Safe – safe – safe," was taking them well out in front. He soon found his stride. The gun brought up from immediately below the bird and the shot taken just as the bird is blotted out had been Mr. Richmond Watson's advice, and it was working. Ten, twelve, thirteen – sixteen, seventeen. He had done well; now the beaters had come to the dip and disappeared, and the drive was almost over.

At that very minute an old cock grouse came skimming towards him over the heather. Out of the corner of his eye Tommy could see the guns to right and left watching. He felt that perhaps they had been too busy to savour his recent peformance to the full. He would show them how to take that first bird far out. Was that not the secret of shooting with two guns? Not a flag to be seen; it was quite safe. He dropped the bird at a gratifyingly long range, and felt pleasantly smug. A moment later the beaters appeared. He turned to his loader. "That makes us eighteen, I think."

Out in front there was a commotion among the beaters. The head keeper was moving towards them. Tommy, feeling the pointing finger of fate, walked out. The head keeper spoke: "It's one of the beaters, Sir. The man never held up his flag and a pellet took him right in the eye." Tommy kept walking, his thoughts a whirl of trains from Inverness and silent luncheons and Workmen's Compensation Acts. He approached the injured party standing in a circle of gawping fellows. The victim turned towards him, and Tommy's knees buckled, for he found himself looking into a blue eye to the left and a gaping socket to the right. Without a word, the wounded man extended an open, grimy hand. It contained a slightly chipped glass eye.

DRUMNADROCHIT

[*For the benefit of the sceptical, the glass eye part of the story is absolutely true.*]

SEEING MOST OF THE GAME
(1942)

The keen shot can learn a great deal, not to speak of getting a lot of amusement, when he is not actually participating in a shoot, but is merely there to watch. When you are shooting, you have no time for looking around at the other guns, with the possible exception of being placed near a dangerous shot! At one time I had a standing invitation to accompany a shoot during the day's proceedings, that is, when I was not there as a gun, which was pretty frequent.

On occasions such as these, you can watch the guns, admire a good working dog and realise what mistakes are being made by the keeper in getting the birds over the guns etc. You wonder how No. 4 can hit anything, considering the ungainly way he stands and holds his gun; and yet he has his percentage of birds down.

Very different is No. 2, who might be a statue by a Greek sculptor, so perfect is his stance and the way he holds his gun: not one unnecessary movement, left arm down the barrels as far as it can stretch and, when he has to take a bird on the side, just an easy swing from the hips, with the minimum of exertion, each muscle playing its part without strain or fuss; and his execution is a joy to watch.

Heavens! No. 6 is going to fire at that rabbit running along the front of the covert; the beaters cannot be more than fifteen or twenty yards from the end of the beat: you hold your breath, expecting a ricochet from a stone to prick one of them; but no squeak from boy or curse from man ensues, so you breathe again.

Out shooting, if there as a gun, you have all too few chances of watching a good dog work – their numbers in comparison with the bad ones and the indifferent are few enough – when you do come cross one, he is well worth watching; except at field-trials, about which there is bound to be a certain artificiality, you seldom have the chance.

Keepers' methods vary considerably in their management of a shoot and their beaters: some are martinets and dragon their beaters like a sergeant of the Guards, and only succeed in rubbing them up the wrong way and making them bad-tempered, thus not being able to get the best out of them. Others are too slack and fail to keep their men in a good line, or allow them to go through the covert too quickly so that the birds rise in clouds over the guns, making it difficult to know which birds to fire at, with the danger of firing at one bird and wounding another.

You can admire the way that individual animals frustrate the designs of the shooters: the sudden swerve of the old cock-pheasant at just the right moment, almost as if he could see the approach of the shot towards him; the sudden twist of the hare, which causes the shot to hit the ground where she should be, but is actually well clear of her as she goes on her way undaunted; the way that woodcock manages to keep tree boles and branches between itself and the nearest gun till it is out of shot. All these things, so interesting to the nature lover, you would miss if you were shooting.

Apart from these considerations, you meet your friends, and go home, grateful to your host and well satisfied with your day's exercise.

LOWLANDER

MENTAL PT AND USEFUL SKILLS
(1964)

When I have temporarily run short of windmills at which to tilt, I blow off my head of steam by railing against the system of education forced on to our fathers, ourselves and our sons. I refer in particular to Latin. Why, in the name of sanity, one should be compelled to imbibe a dead language by stumbling through Caesar's trite despatches is a thing that nobody has ever explained to my satisfaction. The pedagogues say: "It is very useful, being the basis of many modern languages," or "It is an excellent form of mental PT," but neither statement is entirely correct.

And such Latin as was driven into my system in the manner of a medical orderly with a blunt hypodermic needle was never any help to me in absorbing Urdu or Ki-Swahili. Saxon would be a much better basis on which to build up a vocabulary in one's mother tongue. As for mental PT, why not give adolescents a course on income-tax returns or Acol or pools or anything else that would be of subsequent practical benefit?

But schoolmasters never treat one's suggestions for a revised curriculum with the reverence they deserve, having entirely failed to grasp the basic truth that should parents, nuisance though they are, cease to exist, they themselves would soon be unemployed and would have to pass the day in their common-room coffee-housing, presumably, in Latin.

I fear that I shall never see the Golden Age of Education when the time now squandered on that unhandy lingo is used gainfully in teaching boys how to mix cement, make an omelette, mend a puncture, wire a house, dress a bird or knit wood together.

It is the last of these arts that I increasingly covet and my lack of swift skill has never been more obvious than now, when I have had the role of stage-carpenter thrust on to me. Our village yearly gives an old people's party at Christmas, tea being traditionally followed by entertainment. This year it has been decided to present a one-act play, and before I could find an escape I was being told to make a stage set of a hotel passage featuring a bathroom and two bedroom doors.

I refused to have anything to do with what seemed likely to be a vivacious if *risqué* French comedy, but was quelled with a reassurance that it would be good, solid British humour centred on queueing for a morning bath. Anyhow, I was not the Lord Chamberlain, they told me brusquely, and what exactly did I mean by "Dust and derision!"? It would be appreciated if I would direct my energies towards the task of knocking up the scenery and, in the meanwhile, they would excuse me further comments.

It took me a whole day to plan the work, for it had to be made in three identical slabs so that it would go through doors, and it had to reach from the floor to the ceiling. It then took me three more days to make the first section and another three seconds to find out that opening the door could bring the whole structure toppling forward on to the opener.

However, I weighted the back legs with cement blocks and turned my attention to the centre section. Two days later I erected it, to find that it was too tall by half an inch, and after frantic re-measuring realised that the fault lay in the ceiling, which had an imperceptible droop in the centre.

I suppose it will come all right if one works long enough, but it reinforces my belief that the time spent in learning how to decline *mensa* would have been much better used in learning how to make tables and other wooden structures.

Postscript

I seem to put a covey of cats amongst the pigeons by my strictures on the teachings of Latin. How few people recognise persiflage even when laid hot and smoking in front of them! Not for worlds would I suggest any parallel between the clever pedant and head-in-air expert on ablative absolutes, or between the good citizen and the normal person who makes his meaning clear by the use of his mother-tongue; though were such parallels drawn they would confirm Euclid's belief that such lines of thought never meet on common ground.

To every man his preference, and away with regimentation of thought. But let every man recognise that it is only a preference and not a basic requirement of education. To those who hold English all-sufficient I would say "piffle." And to those who overbid the merits of Latin I would answer "Parturient montes nascetur ridiculus mus."

C. C. L. BROWNE

FAME AND THE ROBIN
(1970)

The robin, bird of Christmas cards, probably figures more in British folklore than any other bird. It must be because of the robin's colour and its confidingness. According to legend, the orange-red of its breast, throat and forehead (though the last is seldom noticed except by other robins and ornithologists) is the result of the bird having performed various acts of compassion which included taking water to the souls in Purgatory, whose fires scorched the little brown bird's breast; and of going to the aid of the burning wren on her return from Hell with fire for mankind.

The most popular myth is that the robin's breast was stained with blood when the bird tried to ease the pressure of the crown of thorns while the crossbill (hence its crooked beak) tugged vainly at the nails on that first Good Friday.

Another legendary act of charity performed by the robin was to shroud the babes in the wood with fallen leaves, a task which, according to some, was shared by the wren. In fact, it was once believed that the wren was the robin's wife:

> The robin redbreast and the wren
> Are God Almighty's cock and hen.

John Webster, in *The Duchess of Malfi* (1614), endorsed *The Babes in the Wood* myth:

> Call for the robin red-breast and the wren
> Since o'er shady groves they hover
> And with the leaves and flowers do cover
> The friendless bodies of unburied men.

These stories led to the belief that it is unlucky to harm a robin. What befell the sparrow who killed Cock Robin is not known, but "all the birds of the air" were united in their grief.

Early ornithologists referred to the robin as redbreast but now robin is the usual form. In works of science the names are never combined as they are in Blake's

> A Robin Redbreast in a Cage
> Puts all Heaven in a Rage.

Because young robins have brown speckled breasts until their first moult, some people think that only cock robins are red-breasted. In fact, both sexes are, and both sing. The song is an assertion of territorial claims by individuals of both sexes. This continues from August to December when the birds pair. In spring the cock is an early starter in the dawn chorus. It is a puzzling fact that ownership of territory does not exclude visiting robins from the bird table, which is perhaps neutral ground. The robin's nest, often eccentrically placed, is built by the hen, and she alone incubates the five to six eggs, and the cock feeds her. There are two and sometimes three broods.

The continental robin (*Erithacus rubecula rubecula*) is not so approachable as the British bird (*Erithacus rubecula melophilus*) and is more of a woodland species than ours, which is at home in lanes and gardens. The British robin breeds mainly in the British Isles, but the European, although a winter visitor, breeds solely on the Continent. The aliens have slightly paler breasts than the natives, but they are most easily distinguished by their shyness. The American robin is not a robin but a thrush, and is the bird alluded to in the Negro proverb: "The worm don't hear nothing pretty in the robin's song." In 1908, Lord Northcliffe, after a discussion with Professor Hornaday of the New York Zoological Society, introduced the bird to Sutton Place (now Mr. Paul Getty's home), near Guildford, in the hope that it would establish itself here, but in a letter to the professor seven years later he admitted the failure of his experiment.

Man's affection for the robin is probably atavistic, and originated in the times when he was inadequately equipped to endure the long northern winters. The fact that a small trusting bird, weighing tuppence, should share his hardships and endure until spring gave him comfort. Yet, despite being so frequently depicted in wintry surroundings, the robin is not especially hardy.

There is some conjecture about why the robin is shown on Christmas cards – and only British cards at that. There were no Christmas cards until about 1860 and no reference to the robin's connection with Christmas before that. But postmen in those days wore red uniforms and were nicknamed Robin, just as policemen are called Bobbies today. On the early Christmas cards the robin redbreast was commonly shown carrying a letter. Later the postman's uniform was changed and the link between man and bird was broken; but, as a symbol of Yuletide, the robin continues to this day.

Against competition from the red grouse, the only truly indigenous British species, the robin has become our national bird emblem. Wordsworth unwittingly forecast this in "The Redbreast Chasing a Butterfly":

Art thou the bird whom man loves best
The pious bird with the scarlet breast,
Our little English robin?

MALCOLM MONTEITH

CARDS AT CHRISTMAS
(1940)

What lover of Dickens can ever forget the old-fashioned Christmas card-party at Dingley Dell. That party lives in the memory of all who revere Christmas and its old-established customs; for the custom of playing card games at Christmas is a very old one. Indeed, at one time Christmas was the only season of the year when it was lawful for working men to play at cards; for in 1541 a Statute was passed enacting that husbandmen, artificers, craftsmen, serving men, apprentices, and labourers of all kinds must not play at cards, bowls, quoits, and various other games "out of Christmas"; and even then they could only play these games in the houses or the presence of their masters.

From all that we know of human nature we may suppose that the Statute only increased the practice of card-playing. Certainly there is plenty of evidence to prove that it was a favourite pastime of all classes during the reign of Queen Elizabeth; for the records of the Archdeacons' Visitations are full of references to cases of card-playing on Sunday in all parts of England. And in the *Popische Kingdome* (a translation of the *Regnum Papisticum* of Thomas Naogeorgus), published in 1570, we read that people were encouraged to gamble in church on Christmas Day, because by so doing they would have good luck in play throughout the coming year. The example was probably set by the Queen herself: she was a keen card-player, and Edmund Bohun, whose Character of her was published in 1613, informs us that "especially at Christmas-time she would play Cards and Table, which was one of her usual pastimes; and if at any time she happened to win she would be sure to demand her money" – a trait of character that is typical of the Tudors. Henry VIII was an inveterate gambler, and whenever he lost – which was often – he would fly into a temper.

We may deduce, then, that card-playing was widespread in sixteenth-century England, and that gambling was far more the national vice than drinking. For, about 1576, John Northbrooke, of Bristol, inveighed against dice and cards in his *Spiritus est Vicarius Christi*. In this treatise, attacking "vaine Plays or Enterluds, with other idle Pastimes, etc., commonly used on the Sabboth Day," Northbrooke condemns cards as "the invention of the Devill so that he might the easier bring in Ydolatrie amongst men." And in 1585, Philip Strutte published his Anatomie of Abuses, in which he complained of card-playing on the Sabbath Day, and condemned especially playing at tables, cards, dice, bowls, and the like, when played "for lucre or gaine."

Of far more significance is the fact that in May, 1526, a proclamation was made against all unlawful games "so that in all places Tables, Dice, Cards, and Bowles, were taken and burnt." The result of this proclamation was that the people murmured against Cardinal Wolsey, saying that he grudged every man his pleasure, except his own. Edward Hall, in *The Triumphant Reigne of King Henry the VIII*, states that the proclamation "small tyme endured"; and, indeed, only three years later, Bishop Hugh Latimer delivered his famous *Two Sermons on the Card* at the University of Cambridge on the Sunday before Christmas. The sermons attracted great attention at the time, as well they might, since they drew parallels between the life of a Christian and a game of cards.

The traditional custom between Christmas and cards survived the invective of Northbrooke, Strutte and all the other reformers. From the Annual Register for 1772 we learn that Their Majesties King George III and Queen Charlotte did not attend divine service on Twelfth Day, "their majesties not being accustomed to play at hazard." And in 1831 Lord Chancellor Brougham, addressing the House of Lords, said: "The Archbishop of Canterbury before the last knew the regulations of the Church well, and never suffered a Christmas Day to pass without playing a game of whist, although he was not much attracted to the game."

To-day the custom of playing card games at Christmas is still observed. Every hotel that caters for Christmas visitors includes a whist drive as part of the festivities, and in most families the afternoon of Christmas Day is devoted to playing round games for nuts with the children; and in the evening we elders play bridge, or what in our ignorance imagine to be bridge.

GEORGE F. HERVEY

ALL THINGS BRIGHT AND BEAUTIFUL
(1970)

On the day of the carol concert the junior school hall is puffed with parental pride. The event ushers in the festive season as nothing else does, making real what has hitherto been merely apparent. "Please join in the singing but remain seated," whispers a nervous form master at the door.

The request is unnecessary. Parents squeezed into seats built for infants are quite unable to rise together without causing a pack-of-cards collapse throughout the entire hall where the last odours of lunchtime jam pudding and custard linger amid the Santa Claus mobiles overhead.

Sporting a Fezziwig smile the Headmaster steps forward to welcome everyone, especially the Deputy Mayor, who is wondering how to preserve civic sang-froid while holding a posy. Two hours later he will still be clutching it damply in the back of the mayoral Rolls. With commendable lack of pomp the Narrator enters. His composure is regal. He raises himself to his full three feet ten inches and pipingly declares that what we are about to witness is the annual carol concert performed entirely by the children with words and music provided by them alone.

This is not strictly accurate but nobody cares and all heads swivel as the orchestra of nine-year-olds, some of them in unison, launch into "O little town of Bethlehem." It has a traditional English quality, although composed in America barely one hundred years ago.

By the time the choir is "proclaiming the holy birth" and singing praises "to God and King, and peace to men on earth" the orchestra are in step. The music mistress relaxes visibly. Does one imagine it, or did the pianist mouth to the flautists "F, f, c, f, c, top g, c, top a, g, top a, b flat, long a..."?

But the flautists' eyes are riveted to their music and behind them the clarinets and descant recorders are gaining confidence. An air of rash jauntiness is detected and when a boy trumpeter goes off at an unrehearsed tangent his neighbour stops cutting a swathe through the air with her trombone to fix him with a reproving glance. Giggles from the xylophonist threaten to become infectious. The music mistress stiffens.

A rustle of relief follows the final strains of "Our Lord Immanuel" and the Narrator springs up to lecture sternly on the joys of giving to others. His remarks are illustrated by a short play about Boniface (who has mysteriously chosen a red balaclava to indicate saintliness) and the Christmas Tree. The latter role affords a splendid opportunity for Method acting by an eight-year-old festooned with paper foliage. The leaves, a programme note informs, were made by Class III.

The choir's rendering of the old French carol, "*Entre le boeuf et l'âne gris,*" might disarm a rabid anti-Common Marketeer and a noisy dance sequence about a toy shop explains why members of the orchestra are dressed as puppets. Some fathers even think they recognize favourite shirts and ties missing from the wardrobe in recent weeks. This, presumably, is what the Narrator meant about the joy of giving, even unwittingly.

It is welcome to see the thalidomide boy taking as full a part as he can in a display of reading and movement and instructive to watch how, when he drops his book, it is returned to him unfussily by a matter-of-fact neighbour in pigtails. The lesson in politeness without sentiment, concern without condescension, is salutary.

Salutary, too, perhaps, that the last reading on goodwill to all men should be given by a coloured child who probably cannot spell integration and, as yet, has had no cause to. Perhaps she may never need to learn. At least at Christmas we are entitled to hope so.

LEADING ARTICLE

AN OLD GATE
(1936)

I like that weather-worn old four barred gate
Which no one ever opens. The hedge is old
Each side of it; ash saplings grow behind it,
Their slender boles already ivy-covered
Though they are so much younger than the hedge.
And the gate is ancient, iron-clamped, crooked;
And leads nowhere. That is, leads nowhere now.
Set in an angle of the hedge, it awaits
Final destruction and oblivion.
Its green wood – green with age – will fall apart,
And then be taken to a house for burning,
Or else just left to rot into the ground.
Some more thorn will be planted, the gap closed.
One day bullfinches will be nesting there,
Conspicuous-inconspicuous furtive birds,
Who know the strength of intermatted thorn.
But if I pass alone I shall remember,
When that day comes, that once there was a gate.

N. L. B.